D0588937

Singers & Sweethearts

The Women of Country Music

Singers & Sweethearts

By Joan Dew

A

Country Music
Magazine
Press Book

Dolphin Books

Doubleday & Company, Inc., Garden City, New York, 1977

THE COUNTRY MUSIC MAGAZINE PRESS
PATRICK CARR, EDITOR
CHEH NAM LOW, DESIGNER

ISBN: 0-385-12595-X
LIBRARY OF CONGRESS CATALOG CARD NUMBER 76-54009
COPYRIGHT © 1977 BY KBO PUBLISHERS, INC.
ALL RIGHTS RESERVED
PRINTED IN THE UNITED STATES OF AMERICA
FIRST EDITION

To Cliff, David, and Christopher

CONTENTS

ACKNOWLEDGMENTS

Although writing has been called the loneliest of all professions, no one writes a book, or even a magazine article, entirely alone. Fact-gathering, the most tedious part of a journalist's work, cannot be done successfully without cooperation and help from others. The people who contributed to this book did so in countless ways beyond giving their time in interviews or directing me to new sources of information. Generosity ranging from the loan of a typewriter to transportation to interviews made my away-from-home work infinitely easier. For this, as well as the enthusiasm shown for this project by all who cooperated, I would like to express my deepest gratitude and appreciation.

The following, in alphabetical order, contributed immeasurably to the writing of this book: Lorene Allen, Chet Atkins, Willadeen Blalock, Owen Bradley, Neika Brewer, Mrs. Henry Cannon, Patrick Carr, Barbara Cochran, Cliff Cochran, Hank Cochran, Dottie Cummings, Kelly Delaney, Doug Douglas, Nancy Dunne, Jerry Flowers, Bill Graham, Jack Greene, Juanita Jones, Jim Kemp, John Lentz, Hope Powell, Ray Pradines, George Richey, Susan Roberts, LaWayne Satterfield, Jeannie Seely, Billy Sherrill, Dave Skepner, Marvis Teague and Jim Webb. Special thanks to Mary Ann McCready and to Edna Bloodworth and her staff at Nashville's Spence Manor Hotel.

INTRODUCTION

In 1952, a quiet, unassuming woman stepped before a studio microphone in the old Tulane Motel in Nashville to record a new song. It was called "It Wasn't God Who Made Honky Tonk Angels." Nobody there, least of all the lady herself, Miss Kitty Wells, could have predicted the far-reaching results of that recording session.

The song had been chosen because it was written in answer to a hit single Hank Thompson had out at the time, "Wild Side of Life," which implied that men went astray because God made "honky tonk angels" to lure them into sin. Kitty's rebuttal suggested, in no uncertain terms, that men might regard themselves, not God or women, as responsible for their cheating urges.

The single came out on the Decca label in June. By July, before Kitty was even aware that it had been released, it had hit the charts, and before summer was over it had sold half a million copies. Nobody was more surprised than Kitty, whose only other recording experience had been three years earlier when she'd gone to Atlanta to cut eight gospel songs for RCA Victor. "I was shocked," she remembers. "Women never had hit records in those days. Very few of them ever even recorded. I couldn't believe it had happened."

Before Kitty's breakthrough, "girl singers" had always been a country music afterthought. Women bought most of the records, and it was believed that they would not spend money to hear another woman sing. The few females who did record sang religious or cowboy songs, like Patsy Montana's "I Wanna Be a Cowboy's Sweetheart." Love songs, cheatin' songs, drinkin' songs, heartbreak songs, were all written and sung by men, expressing the male viewpoint. But in "It Wasn't God Who Made Honky Tonk Angels," a *woman* was telling the female's side of the story for the first time. The fans loved it.

Record labels weren't the only ones discriminating against girl singers before Miss Kitty came along and added a new dimension to country music: Bookers were equally unimpressed. In the forties any woman (other than country comedienne Minnie Pearl or the distaff side of the Original Carter Family) appearing on a stage was there simply to look sweet and fill in the breaks between male singers.

"Girl singers had no identity of their own, no music of their own," Minnie Pearl remembers. "They'd sing a popular song of the day—assuming one of the men didn't want to sing it—and they'd usually yodel. But the industry didn't take them seriously.

They were fluffed off by everyone."

Minnie, who was the first female star of country music, had been traveling on the road for ten years before any solo woman singer showed up on the "Opry Circuit." Even then they were paid almost nothing—forty or fifty dollars a week—and they had to take care of their own expenses, Minnie says. "I remember in 1949 the Prince Albert Tobacco Company took a country show on tour to Europe, and not one girl singer was asked to come along. There was Red Foley, Roy Acuff, Hank Williams, Jimmie Dickens and myself. On some of the shows Red's wife, Eva, and Hank's wife, Audrey, got up and sang, but they were just there along with their husbands, not as performers. None of us had any idea then that women would some day be among the giants of the industry."

Chet Atkins, RCA Division Vice President in charge of Nashville operations, says that women got such a slow start because labels had no faith in them as potential money-makers. "You know record companies," he says dryly, "they'll record a mule braying if they think it will sell. It wasn't because they had any prejudice against women, they just didn't think they could make any money off them. No one ever had in the past, and in those days women were confined by conformity. But the minute Kitty Wells proved women could sell records, we all went out looking for girl singers."

"In those days I wouldn't have believed women would sell records either," Minnie admits. "The women who bought the records sat home next to a pot-bellied, beer-drinking husband and daydreamed about being with Eddy Arnold or Ernest Tubb, Hank Williams or Roy Acuff. They had romantic images of these men and sexual fantasies about them that offered escapism from their day-to-day existence. You would never have convinced me then that a woman could headline a show and pull huge crowds of other women, or sell them millions of records. I thought they would resent another woman up there singing to them, or feel she was some kind of competition.

"But then, after World War II, things began to change. Women began getting fed up with their way of life. They started to push against it and when they heard songs, that reinforced these feelings, or songs of love told from a woman's point of view, they identified with it and they went out and bought the records."

Today dozens of big-selling, headlining artists in country music are women. Barbara Mandrell, Jeannie Seely, Lynn Anderson, Dottie West, Jessi Colter, Connie Smith, Barbara Fairchild, Donna Fargo, Brenda Lee, Jody Miller, Jeanne Pruett, Susan Raye, Jeannie C. Riley, Mary Lou Turner and newcomers La Costa and Crystal Gayle are just some of the women who sell records and star in concerts.

But there are five whose success in the industry stands out above all the others. They are Loretta Lynn, a Kentucky coal miner's daughter who inherited Kitty Wells' title of the Queen of Country Music; Tammy Wynette, a Mississippi farm girl whose records have sold more than any other woman in her field; Dolly Parton, one of the most talented and prolific songwriters in any music; June Carter Cash, daughter of one legend, wife of another, songwriter, singer and actress, and Tanya Tucker, dynamic young innovator who reached stardom long before adulthood.

Even if they were merely "girl singers," criss-crossing the United States 250 to 300 days a year in luxurious custom-designed buses to take their music to the fan's front door, these women would still be a fascinating group—all from poor backgrounds, now millionaires; all with one foot solidly planted in demanding careers while the other remains just as firmly rooted to home and family; all deeply proud of country music and their position in it, but also proud of one another and sharing a strong, invisible bond most females in other fields of show business, from rock music to acting, don't even know exists.

They come and go with a freedom of movement most women can only fantasize. Their homes and families revolve around *their* schedules, even when they are away. On many levels they are much more liberated than their urban feminist sisters, yet they are doggedly bound by tradition, and much of their thinking would be considered "old-fashioned" by today's standards.

Each has her own little hive where she is Queen Bee, and each has leverage in her industry (they all own related businesses such as publishing and booking agencies) which is both recognized and respected. Yet money, power or status was never the goal for any of them. Rather, it is a side-effect (sometimes pleasing, sometimes perplexing) of other drives, other ambitions.

They live their music, but they don't always live up to it. (Loretta, who sings "Don't Come Home A'Drinkin' With Lovin' On Your Mind," has been living with a husband who, she implies, does exactly that, since she was thirteen; Tammy, who sings "Stand By Your Man," has left four husbands.) Yet their fans understand the contradictions and know the women are singing from the heart even if they can't always apply it to their own lives.

Eighty per cent of country records are still bought by women and ninety per cent of the appeal of country music is in the lyrics. The record buyers pay close attention to the words, and through their music these stars touch, influence and comfort their fans with themes that say "marital problems, longing and heartbreak are no different for me than they are for you. Some things don't change no matter how much money you earn."

Minnie Pearl's observation that at one time she thought female audiences would consider an attractive girl singer a competitive threat prompts a closer look at the sexual image these women project. In appearance they range from very attractive to knock-out beautiful; in age from eighteen to forty-seven. All are well-built, all are frankly flirtatious, though each has her own style. Yet they have as many, if not more, women fans than men, simply because there's not a femme fatale among them. Loretta is everybody's sister. Tammy's vulnerability evokes sympathy. Dolly makes sex funny. Like Mae West, she's a caricature, not to be taken seriously. June is *Mrs.* Johnny Cash, and Tanya, for all her lusty lyrics, is a tomboyish teen-ager.

But what of the women behind the images? How real are they? What excites them? What frightens them? Do they enjoy their fame and fortune? Do they like each other? Do they like themselves? How do they feel about their roles as career women, wives, mothers, lovers, business executives? Do they worry about the future? Regret the past? These are among the questions I began asking in 1973 when I was first sent to Nashville on assignment from a national magazine to profile some of the outstanding women in country music.

The more I learned, the more intrigued I became and the less I felt I knew about them. They certainly didn't resemble any stars I had ever met in fifteen years of interviewing celebrities in Hollywood and New York, but the explanation for that difference did not lie in their rural backgrounds. I had met many stars with country roots and humble beginnings, but in temperament and presence they were essentially no different from celebrities raised in ghettos or wealthy suburbs.

These country stars had attained the pinnacle of success in their field, winning peer acclaim, fan adulation and earning millions, yet in certain areas—such as ego and attitude—they remained so untouched by their status that it was as though nobody had gotten around to telling them they were superstars. In other areas of show business stars do on occasion remain humble at the top, but they are never unaware of the power they hold, the authority they wield. These women, however, were either oblivious to or totally disinterested in this fringe benefit of stardom. All of them, for example, could afford as much personal service help as they wanted, yet none were waited on, fussed over or pampered, not because they weren't aware that way of life was available to them, but because it held no appeal.

Over the years, each time I returned to Nashville on subsequent magazine assignments or met one of them somewhere on the road to travel on their buses from show to show, something would come up that would prompt me to think, "Ah ha, so that's it. Now I'm getting the real picture." But before that conclusion could be verified, something else would happen to completely contradict my smug analysis.

So in many ways (wonderful ways) these women still remain a mystery to me. I have tried here to present the information and observations that in my opinion most clearly define them mentally, emotionally and musically, but I am not presumptious enough to think all the layers of complexity have been stripped away. The private inner core remains intact and untouched, and for that I do not apologize. It's one of the things that makes them unique, unpredictable, and fascinating.

Joan Dew
Calabasas, California, January 1977

Singers & Sweethearts

"If I had it to do all over again, I wouldn't."

LORETTA

Kitty Wells paved the way for woman-to-woman "message music" when she sang "It wasn't God Who Made Honky Tonk Angels" in 1952, but it wasn't until a decade later that the fans found their real Pied Piper. Loretta Lynn was her name, and she sang to and about the frustrations of millions of blue-collar housewives, women who didn't want independence from a man so much as a man they could depend on. Loretta's pure, strong, soulful voice hit them from their radios, and Loretta was here to stay.

"Don't come home a-drinkin' with lovin' on your mind," was one of Loretta's messages, and as Minnie Pearl notes, "Loretta sang what these women were thinking." Loretta sang about men who fooled around, having a good time for themselves while their wives stayed at home changing diapers, wiping noses, and scrimping enough to make it out of the grocery store every week. Within a remarkably short time, she had become the spokeswoman for every woman who had gotten married too early, gotten pregnant too often, and felt trapped by the tedium and drudgery of her life. Betty Freidan and Gloria Steinem couldn't reach these women; Loretta, who expressed her disinterest in 'the movement' by falling asleep in Betty Freidan's presence on *The David Frost Show*, could. Her message was straightforward and practical: "We know we can't leave the farms, can't abandon our children, can't all have careers, can't even get out of the kitchen—but we *can* show our men that what's fair for the goose is fair for the gander, and we have just as much right to get some fun out of life as they do." While Tammy Wynette, ever the romanticist, was singing "Stand By Your Man," Loretta was saying "stand up to your man."

The fans knew that Loretta was singing from personal experience. They knew songs like "Don't Come Home A-Drinkin' " and "You Ain't Woman Enough To Take My Man" were aimed directly at her husband, Mooney ("Doo") Lynn. She had lived it, too. She was one of them, and that gave her the right to speak for all of them.

As a result, Loretta's fans are like no others. They share an unprecedented, unbreakable bond with her, as well as with one another. They don't just love her; they worship her. This phenomenon cannot be fully appreciated unless one travels on the road with Loretta to the places *her* people live—rural areas, factory towns, farm centers—the

areas where she represents a paradoxical combination of idol and intimate, goddess and girlfriend, queen and commoner.

They come in droves, often bringing their children and brown-bag lunches, arriving hours before show time to get the best seating. They also bring their old, their sick, their crippled and maimed, as though simply being in the light of Loretta's presence will help their psyches, if not heal their bodies. At times her concerts take on the air of an evangelistic faith-healing meeting, with fans calling out her name and the songs they want to hear as fervently (and sometimes as reverently) as a sinner calling to the Lord.

The outsider, who immediately feels like a stranger at a family reunion, observes it all with a mixture of awe and uneasiness. It is spooky, and somehow sad, and yet terribly exciting.

Loretta is not aware of the power she holds over these people, and if asked about it the question isn't clear to her: "What power? They know I'm one of them and that's why they like me."

She proves she's one of them by talking to them from the stage as though they were family sitting around her living room: "If I can't hit the high notes tonight, it's 'cause I got a sore throat, so just bear with me." "Tell me, can y'all see through this dress? I couldn't find my long slip and them boys in the band say you can't see nothin', but I don't trust them a lick." "This is yore show. Just call out whatever you wanna hear and if I got the strength, I'll sing it."

Her audiences eat it up. They run to the stage throughout the concert to flash their Instamatics; they cheer and whistle and stomp and applaud for more, and when it's all over they stand in line to get her autograph on programs and albums they've bought earlier from her bandmembers. While she writes her name until her hand begins to tremble, they ask questions: "Is Mooney with you on this trip?" "How are the twins?" They make comments: "That's a pretty dress." "You're looking better now that you put on a little weight." They confide intimate and sometimes heart-breaking problems: "Our boy lost his leg in an accident. Will you send him a note?" "My husband has another woman, and I don't know what to do about it." ("Fight for him, honey, if he's worth it. If he ain't, let him go," she advises, and amazingly the woman appears consoled.)

Only after she's been led back to the bus by her driver-bodyguard, Jim Webb, does the crowd begin to file out toward the exits. They're still exhilarated, but they've left her exhausted and drained, as though they've sapped her strength and are taking it home with them. On the bus she heads straight to her private compartment in the rear. She closes the door behind her, shutting out the world until the next town, the next show, the next audience.

Loretta owns 3,700 acres of prime Tennessee countryside surrounding a two-story, white-columned authentic antebellum mansion right out of 'Gone With The Wind.' But she lives in the back of a bus. Granted, it's a luxurious, custom-designed, $160,000 MC 8 Challenger, forty feet

Components of the Loretta Lynn life: Above, she clowns with husband Mooney Lynn outside their genuine antebellum Southern mansion; near left, she leaves her bus, the back compartment of which is her true home; far left, she takes her place as one of country music's modern generation of women superstars. With her are (left to right) Lynn Anderson, Dolly Parton, Dottie West and Tammy Wynette.

long and plushly decorated, but it is still a bus and not the place most people would choose to spend two-thirds of their life.

Other country artists use their buses as a convenient, comfortable mode of transportation from one-nighter to one-nighter, criss-crossing the country with their bands in privacy and luxury, with refrigerators, cooking facilities, the latest in stereo equipment, television and comfortable sleeping quarters. The buses also serve as dressing rooms when they arrive at their destinations—auditorium, fairground or arena—where there is often nothing more than a public toilet for stars to change and wait between shows. Loretta's bus serves as all of this, and more. Whereas other performers check into motels daily, even if it's just for a few hours before a show, Loretta stays on her bus days at a time without leaving it except to go on stage.

When band members Don Ballinger, Dave Thornhill, Bob Hempker, Gene Dunlap, Chuck Flynn and Ken Riley get off to eat or stretch their legs at a truck stop, Loretta remains safely hidden in the privacy of her back compartment, a room that never sees the outside world because the black-out curtains are closed at all times. She says she got in the habit of drawing the drapes years ago when several threats were made on her life. Now they are kept closed because she likes it that way. In this eight by ten space with a dressing table, two chairs, a sofa that becomes a bed, and a table, she eats, sleeps, listens to music, watches television, daydreams, talks all night long to a friend if there's one along, and revels in being alone when there isn't. Up front, in the lounge area, her 'boys' (and her son, Ernest Ray, who sings on the show) play poker, watch the countryside fly by, swap outrageous tales and generally have a merry time. But Loretta seldom joins them, and when she does it's for no more than a few minutes at a time.

Back in her compartment there's a strange dissociation from time and place. There is no night or day, no sunshine, moonlight or rain, no cities, no countryside, just the steady drone of the powerful engine and the rolling vibration of the big wheels beneath her. Even the awareness of motion is dimmed by the blacked-out windows so that it's more like being in a motorized cocoon than a moving vehicle. When it's time to go on stage she asks her driver, "Where are we?" so she won't make the embarrassing mistake of saying, "It's great to be back in Syracuse" when she's really in Harrisburg.

Loretta has lived this way for close to a decade now. "Sometimes I feel like a monkey in a closed cage," she once said. "They take me out to do my act, then put me back in until the next town." But at other, more introspective times, she admits she has grown so accustomed to her lifestyle that she feels "restless and nervous" when she's away from it for long.

When asked why she imprisons herself this way, she gives an excuse she has undoubtedly come to believe. "If I try to get off the bus to eat, fans won't let me alone. It makes it hard for the boys to enjoy their meal, and impossible for me."

Certainly when she pulls into a truck stop in a huge bus with her name emblazoned on the sides in three-foot letters, she is bound to get attention from the truckers inside the cafe. But when you're worth five million dollars you can buy the freedom to move about if you really want it. There are few restaurants in this country where Loretta couldn't eat unmolested and probably unrecognized if the bus was parked discreetly out of sight down the street.

When Loretta does spend the night in a motel she remains on the bus until Jim has checked her into a room. She then goes there like a dutiful child, never leaving it again until it's time to get back on the bus. She has been in every state and most of our cities, but all she's seen is the rooms of their Holiday Inns and the stages of their auditoriums.

Most people would find living this way morbidly depressing. Loretta does not. "I don't ever get tired of the back room of my bus," she says. "I'd rather be there than anywhere else, except on stage."

Why, Loretta?

"Because nobody can bother me back there. I wouldn't have thought of myself as a loner, growing up in a big family, then going right from that to a family of my own, but I guess that's

Loretta and Mooney Lynn, married couple. When they married, she was still a child and he was a man of the world. Now, she is the star of the household while he takes care of the farm. It is a notoriously difficult relationship, but Loretta swears she will never quit.

what I am. I love to be alone. Even when I'm on the farm I sneak off down to this little log cabin we got and sit there by myself and just think about things, or write songs."

"Loner" would probably be the last word friends would use to describe Loretta. She attracts people like metal dust to a magnet. She is warm, witty, guileless and totally without pretension, as open and candid on the first encounter as she would be on the fiftieth. Her instincts are infallable and her insight uncanny, and at times it's almost as though she reads minds (she says her mother has this same "gift"). This makes it difficult, if not impossible, to get around Loretta. She may appear casual and easy-going, but her mind's eye watches constantly and if she misses something it's usually because it didn't happen.

She can be as playful as a child one minute, troublesome and suspicious the next. She mothers men (her band-members call her 'mom') and respects women ("Any woman who don't stick up for other women is stupid," she says). She is fiercely proud, stubborn and determined. If she sets out to do something, she can't rest until she's done it. Attaining goals, she says, "is simply mind over matter. And I mind what matters."

She can and does laugh at herself. But she does not take unfair criticism without retaliation. Her record producer, Owen Bradley, tells of a tour in England where a reviewer referred to her as 'the toothy Loretta Lynn.' (Loretta is very sensitive about her overbite, although her mouth is actually very attractive.) "The fella's name was Peter somebody and from the stage she said 'If that *Pee-tah* is here I wanna meet him, 'cause I'm gonna whup him over the whole state of England!'"

Bradley keeps a book at his recording studio, Bradley's Barn, of 'Loretta-isms,' words and phrases she comes up with that are uniquely her own. She once explained the difference between a fiddle and a violin to him this way: "A fiddle is a fiddle, but a whole bunch of fiddles is a violin." Half a tone higher is "Half a hair [pronounced har] higher"; one night she needed "smelling sauce" and someone had "very close veins." She wanted to "rememberize" her song and she knew

someone who talked "high-kaflutin'."

Lorene Allen, Loretta's good friend and the office manager at Loretta Lynn Enterprises, says her boss's generosity and genuine love of people are her most endearing qualities and her biggest shortcomings. "She can't say 'no' because she wants to help anyone who asks," Lorene explains. "Consequently she makes promises she can't keep because there are only so many hours in the day. I've never seen Loretta turn away from anyone. She considers them all her friends."

By now Loretta's background is well-known. She is the second of eight children born to a coal miner and his wife during the Depression in Butcher's Hollow, Kentucky, an area so remote there were no roads leading to the cabins, and so pitch black at night torches were required to light the way home. The "holler" was home to twelve families, mostly Butchers and Webbs (Loretta was a Webb), all of them related, all of them dirt poor. The families had lived there as long as anyone could remember. No one ever moved away. The women married young, had babies one after the other, and worked from dawn till late at night doing the endless backbreaking chores required of them as wives and mothers: chopping wood for fireplaces and wood-burning stoves, scrubbing clothes on a washboard, boiling diapers, planting vegetables, hoeing and harvesting, canning, sewing, milking and churning (if they were lucky enough to own a cow), making soap from lye and hog fat, hauling water from the well or the creek, cooking—all this and more while caring for babies that seldom arrived more than a year apart.

The men worked in the coal mine. Loretta's father, who bore a striking resemblance to her favorite movie star, Gregory Peck, worked the night shift. He'd come in black and grimy from coal dust about the time his wife and children were getting up to start the day. He'd sleep with noisy kids tumbling around him until afternoon, then help with the heavier chores, like chopping wood and hoeing, until time to head back to the mines at sundown.

Their diet consisted of what vegetables they could grow and bread and gravy. They rarely had meat, and Loretta remembers her mother eating

Showbiz couple: Mooney the farmer and Loretta the star. The event is a Conway Twitty Muscular Dystrophy benefit.

Loretta and the high life. Above, she hoots with fellow country star Tommy Overstreet at one of Conway Twitty's Muscular Dystrophy benefits. On the right, she boards a Government helicopter.

sugar in grease when she craved sweets. There were no luxuries whatsoever, and conveniences like electricity and indoor plumbing were non-existant. It reads like a grim way to live, but both Loretta and her mother, Mrs. Tom Butcher, remember it as the happiest of times. "We were so far below the poverty level we didn't know there was one," Loretta laughs. "We had no contact with the outside world, and everybody we knew was just as poor as we was. I never had any urge to get out of there, never thought I would, if I thought about it at all. I had wonderful parents. Mommie was sweet and good, and the prettiest woman I ever saw. And my Daddy—well, he rocked me in a rocking chair right up to the time I got married. He always had three or four of us kids in his lap. I was a Daddy's girl for sure. I never saw him do nothing wrong or raise his voice to Mommie. You could tell how much they loved each other just by the way he'd put his arm around her shoulder some times."

"We didn't have time to worry," says Mrs. Butcher, a tiny, fragile-looking woman with enormous black eyes, who now lives in Wabash, Indiana with her second husband. "We had too much work to do for that. But we had fun too. Loretta's Daddy, who died just two years before she started singing, had a good disposition and he loved his children. We liked to sing and dance. Loretta was the show-off. She always wanted to be the center of attention. She made us laugh and kept us entertained. She'd sing so loud her Daddy would tell her to quiet down or she'd wake up the whole holler, and she'd just laugh and sing louder.

"All the kids had chores, but Loretta, who was the oldest girl, mostly helped take care of the littler kids. Couldn't trust her to wash dishes cause she'd hide 'em under the sink cupboard so

On the facing page, Loretta when she first made it in the music business, fresh from very young motherhood and a farm labor job. Top left, she cuts a track with Ernest Tubb, her first duet partner (behind the microphone on the right of the photo). Top right, she escorts soldiers through Nashville's Hall of Fame museum. Above, she sings with the Wilburn Brothers, on whose TV show she was a regular and with whom she would later fight a long battle over ownership of her song rights.

she could get back out to play. But she loved to sit and rock the babies and sing to them."

Loretta's mother is half Indian (her grandfather was a full-blooded Cherokee) and half Irish, but her personality reflects more of the quiet Indian dignity than the fiery Irish temperament. Loretta, though, inherited her mother's portion of the latter. Even as a child she was headstrong and feisty. Had she been a quiet, docile, obedient little girl she might not be the Queen of Country Music today, because she wouldn't have married Mooney Lynn against her parents wishes. He was a 21-year-old veteran from the next "holler" over who came home from World War II ready to find a wife. The fact that Loretta was only thirteen didn't bother him a bit.

"You gotta understand girls mature faster back in the hills," he explains. "I knew I wanted Loretta as soon as I saw her on the school yard playing ring-around-the-rosie. I had only visited her house twice when I went home and told my mother I was gonna marry her."

When Loretta told her parents she intended to marry Mooney they were distraught. "I begged and pleaded and cried," Mrs. Butcher remembers, "and her Daddy walked the floor and cried. We both knew there wasn't no use to tell her she *couldn't* do it, because she would have run off with him anyway. I was too upset to go down to Paintsville and see them get married. I just stayed home and cried."

Loretta got pregnant on her honeymoon, but didn't know it for several months, until she began feeling "funny" and her stomach started protruding. She went to the doctor who explained the facts of life (her Daddy had always told her babies were found under cabbage leaves) and assured her that as long as a wife "slept" with her husband, this was bound to happen.

"She was still a child herself," Mrs. Butcher recalls. "Why, I looked out the window one day when she was visiting me and she was out there climbing a tree with her brothers, and her seven months gone pregnant! Scared me to death. But even as young as she was, she was always a good mother. She'd had plenty of practice on her little brothers and sisters."

Within five years Loretta had four babies of her own to care for—Betty Sue, Cissy, Jack and Ernest Ray. Mooney had moved his family to Custer, Washington, where he worked as a logger and a mechanic while Loretta planted and picked berries, took care of the children, helped cook for the field hands and cleaned house for their landlord so they could live rent-free.

"When I married Doo it was like stepping out of one world into another," she says. "Mommie and Daddy were very close. They talked over everything. Doo hadn't been raised like that. His folks fought a lot. His mother divorced his father three times and married him four. I guess the reason she kept going back to him was 'cause she had ten kids by him and they needed a daddy. Doo was the oldest, so he was used to bossing his sisters and brothers around, and when he married me he treated me like one of the kids. My Daddy was a gentle man. Marrying Doo was like going from a kind father to a strict one. After we had kids of our own Doo would take a belt to me as quick as he would to one of them. Now, I can see it's just how he was raised, 'cause I know he loves me. But back then I was too resentful to think about that. It's funny how it's the old hurts that never heal.

"I still remember how much it hurt when he sent me back home to my folks after we'd been married just a few months. This was before we knew I was pregnant. He had his brother take me home at ten o'clock one night because he said I couldn't cook worth a durn. 'Course he was right 'bout that . . . I'd left home too young to learn—but it hurt me so much that it ate at me for weeks. I had started getting over it when I found out I was pregnant. By then he was begging me to come back, and with a baby on the way . . . well, what was I to do?

"It was hard for me to leave Butcher's Hollow and my family and travel so far away to live. I'd never been further than Paintsville, ten miles from home, in my life. But it helped our marriage 'cause I couldn't run home crying to Mommie everytime something went wrong.

"After a while I got to liking it in Washington. I was the fastest strawberry picker in the county.

They finally brought in a nineteen-year-old Mexican boy who outpicked me, but he didn't pick the berries as clean as I did. I hoed berries too, so I worked in the fields from late Spring to early Fall. I took the kids with me and spread 'em on a blanket while I worked. I took them with me when I cleaned house too, 'cause I sure couldn't afford no babysitter. Our house was owned by Clyde and Bob Green, and they needed someone to clean their house 'cause the aunt who lived with them was in her eighties and couldn't do heavy work. Her name was Blanche Smith and she was like a mother to me for eleven years. She taught me how to cook and we made three meals a day for the help together."

Loretta had been married for twelve years and her youngest child was already in school when Mooney got the idea to get her on a show at the local grange hall.

"The grange hall was like a farmer's co-op," Mooney says, "where you could take the family on Friday and Saturday nights. The kids played in the basement while the grown-ups drank beer and danced and listened to music. A bunch of us couples used to hang around down there and I told them Loretta could sing as good as the girls on the radio. I had bought her this little guitar for her birthday and she had learned to play it, so I asked the band leader if she could sing with them and he said 'yes.' They all liked her singing, and that made me real proud. Before long she'd been offered a seven-night-a-week job at a real club and we'd gotten together a little band of our own."

During that first year in show business, Loretta was torn between excitement and terror. "I was scared to death to get up and sing in front of people. The only thing that gave me the nerve was Doo making me mad, calling me a 'dumb hillbilly' when I said I couldn't do it. But I also thought it was fun working in a club and meeting all the people. I'd been a housewife since I was thirteen and had never gotten out like that before."

Within a few months Mooney had traveled to Tacoma and persuaded Buck Owens to let Loretta sing on his television show, which was broadcast to Canada. Norm Burley, a lumber tycoon from Vancouver, saw the show, thought she had potential, and offered to send Mooney and Loretta to Hollywood so they could record a song she'd written. Burley financed the pressing of 3500 singles, and Loretta mailed them out to disc jockeys all across the country from a list given to her by a radio station. Deejays played "I'm a Honky Tonk Girl," listeners requested it, juke box owners bought it, Loretta and Mooney toured the country in a beat-up Mercury to promote it, and the unheard-of happened: The record made it to number fourteen on the charts. Before anybody got around to telling them it's not done that way, Loretta and Mooney had already done it. They were headed for Nashville, a Decca contract, and the Grand Ole Opry.

"It all happened so *fast*," Mooney says, in a tone that implies he still can't quite believe it. "We never had time to really sit down and think about it before Loretta was already on her way to the top.

"Lord, in the beginning all I had in mind was for her to do a little singing around Washington for a few extra dollars. We thought it was great when she got ten dollars for a night. It was kinda fun, but the furtherest my thinking ever went was that if she got a few breaks, maybe she could record some. I knew absolutely nothing about the business, or how much money was in it. If somebody had told me I wouldn't have believed them." Nor would he have believed that a few years later his wife would be the biggest female star in country music and *he'd* be the one staying home with the kids while *she* went out and brought home the bacon.

Mooney has often been painted as a dictatorial, domineering bully, a crude, unsympathetic and arrogant man. Undoubtedly he may have been all of these at times, but you wouldn't know it sitting with him alone in a quiet hotel room where he talks of his wife and marriage with tenderness and concern. At nearly fifty he still has a boyish face, but his eyes are old, and usually bloodshot. He smiles easily and blushes when he tells something embarrassing on himself. His hands fidget. He's nervous talking to an outsider, not too confident, but not afraid either, too proud to evade

Above, Loretta on stage, where she is a strange mixture of queen and confidante. Right, she stays behind signing autographs after a show, as she always does (even if collapsing). Far right, she rehearses while Mooney chats with Conway Twitty, with whom she has recorded (and still records) some of the most successful duets in country music.

questions, too stubborn to lie. This is a man who threw out a hook on a ten-pound test line and pulled in a whale that promptly swallowed him. He's been living in the belly of that whale ever since, and the adjustment has not been easy.

"When I first realized what was happening to Loretta, it scared me to death. At first, you know, you can't see it 'cause you're too close to it and you're working, going all the time. Then one day it hits you. 'God a-mighty, what have I done? Here I had this sweet, pretty little wife, a good homemaker, wonderful mother to our children, and the next thing you know I've got a *star!*' It wasn't her fault. She didn't ask to get in it. That was my idea. But once she was in it, she took to it like she was born for it.

"Loretta and I were always together a lot in the old days. She liked the outdoors as much as I did. She was a great cook . . . could cook a better meal on two dollars than most women on ten. She made everything from scratch. And she had fun with her kids. They never got on her nerves. I was very proud of her. We didn't have much, but I thought we had a pretty good life. Then I saw all that slipping away. Don't get me wrong. I love the money we have now. I'd be a fool and a liar if I said I didn't. But I'd give anything in the world if we could go back to like it was, and still have some of the money. But you can't have both. And there's no going back. Life don't work that way.

"A couple of times I came close to asking her to quit. But I knew if she did she'd be miserable, 'cause she'd had a taste of it then. It was in her blood. It gets in their blood, you know, like dope, or a disease. And Loretta's the type of person that no matter what she does she wants to do it the best. So once she got started, if she hadn't been allowed to take it all the way to the top, it would have killed her. Now she lives to entertain those people. The money don't mean nothing to her. She's never been a big money spender. But I've seen her when she was wore out from traveling, sick with a cold or the flu and just about on her last leg. And she'd walk out there on a stage and that applause . . . well, no doctor in the world could give her medicine that would do her near as much good."

Most husbands of stars find living off their wives' income the most difficult adjustment. Mooney was no exception. "It was real hard at first because I had always been the provider, and done it with my own two hands 'cause that's all I knew, so when people started saying 'Mr. Loretta Lynn' it would really get to me. But bless Loretta, she made that a lot easier. The money was a tender subject with me, but when it come up she would say, 'If you hadn't started me, helped me and been behind me, we wouldn't be making all this money, so you've earned it as much as I have.' So she made me feel like I had contributed. And of course I'm proud of her and her success and proud to be her husband.

"Since we've had the farm I feel like that's my

part of the work now. If I go out and buy a pair of mules for $1500 and trade them for $2500, I feel like I've really done something great. I know that can't compare to Loretta making $15,000 in one night, but for me it's just as big a thrill. I can't lay down on work. I'd go crazy. I've worked all my life. And I'm not a very good supervisor, so if there's a fence needs mending at home, or a tractor needs fixin', I get out and do it. I take a lot of pride in that place."

The fact that Loretta doesn't share Mooney's pride and interest in the farm is a point of contention in their marriage, especially since she's the one who wanted it so badly. When they bought the farm in 1967 they really couldn't afford it. But when Loretta saw it, it was love at first sight and she was determined to have it.

"We'd been out driving, looking at another piece of property near Nashville, and we got lost coming back," she remembers. "We rounded a bend on this old dirt road, and there up on a hill

sat this beautiful old southern mansion, just like Scarlett O'Hara's house. There was a mill and a millstream across the road with pretty trees and a mossy bank leading down to the water, and it looked like the most peaceful place on earth. I told Mooney we *had* to get it."

"They wanted $250,000 for the place, including the cattle and the tractor," Mooney recalls, "and they insisted on $80,000 down. All we had in the world was $10,000, so I went to our bank to see if they'd loan us the balance with Loretta's lifetime recording contract as collateral. They turned us down. I found another bank just a few days before escrow was supposed to close. I was so worried about getting the money that I really hadn't checked the old place good. The day after we got it I crawled under the house because I'd seen a sag in the parlor and I thought maybe something had broken loose. Nobody had lived in the place for twelve years. The house was supported by eighteen-inch, hand-hewn oak beams

Loretta's holdings, seldom visited, include a nice herd of horses on her dude ranch.

and they looked okay. I was laying under there on my back, trying to figure out what was causing the sag, and I lifted my leg up and kicked at one of those beams. The damn thing crumbled right in two under my foot, rotted through from termites. A bushel of that dried old brown honeycomb fell on me, and I lay there and cried like a baby. Then I got my cigarette lighter out and debated about burning the dadburned place down. But then I thought, 'Hell, as hard as Loretta works and as bad as she wants this place, I'll fix up the sonofabitch if it kills me.' That was ten years ago, and I ain't done yet!

"I couldn't get nobody to go under the house with me to re-build the foundation 'cause it was too dangerous. So I cut down trees for the beams and drug 'em under there and mixed my concrete and poured it for support. It took me six months of working under there every day to get the house safe enough to move my family in. We've put four times as much as we paid for it into fixing it up,

and we're still making improvements.

"It's a beautiful, valuable place now, and me and the babies love it. But Loretta, well she comes in off the road and she's tired and she don't pay much attention to what's been going on there. I want to show off things I've done and take her out and show her the cattle, stuff like that, and she wants to talk about the crowds at her last show, or some song she's gonna record. She loves the road; I can't take it. I love the farm; she gets restless there after a few days. We really live in two different worlds."

Loretta says the same thing in a different way: "Mooney and me have about as much in common as liquor and lovin'. I don't care about his old cows and he don't care about what's going on in my work. Oh, when I need his advice he's always there to give it, and I do ask his opinion on anything that's important because I trust his judgement more'n anybody else's. But what I'm saying is, we don't have anything to talk about. If we

The little Tennessee town of Hurricane Mills also belongs to Loretta, who has a large payroll.

Mooney Lynn with the twins at home. Loretta was on the road most of the time while the twins were growing, and so Mooney became "both father and mother" to them. The resulting issues of loyalty and guilt are a considerable source of friction in the family.

talk about our older kids there's always something he's mad about with one of 'em. If we talk about the babies, the twins, I get upset 'cause it reminds me of what I'm missing by being away all the time. So mostly we talk about what we'll do in the future, when I slow down. Or we don't talk at all."

The twins, Patsy and Peggy, are another source of contention between Loretta and Mooney. They were born twelve years ago when Loretta's career was just beginning to build momentum. Had she stopped then to stay home with them for a few years, she would not have become the star she is today because that all-important timing would have been lost irretrievably. They both decided it would be wiser for her to continue on the road while Mooney spent more time at home supervising their upbringing. The result is that he has been both mother and father to the girls.

Loretta suffers over this more than any other single factor in her life. She feels enormous guilt because her duties as a mother have been fulfilled by someone else; she is hostile about being "pushed out of the nest" and denied the privileges of motherhood she so enjoyed with her first four children, and she is jealous over the fact that the twins are obviously closer to their father than they are to her.

This last factor is Mooney's lever, and although it may be an unconscious act on his part, he uses it. On one of her rare evenings at home he will say to the girls (who are usually draped around him watching TV), "Now don't ya'll forget to kiss yore Mama goodnight," and an observer can see the fleeting look of pain cross Loretta's face.

Mooney is aware that Loretta feels cheated because she hasn't been around to watch the twins, who are bright, cute and precocious, develop into adolescence. But trying to reassure her by saying he's always taught the girls to love and respect her only makes matters worse. She's resentful that he feels he *has* to do that. "It's a funny deal. In country music we're always singing about home and family. But because I'm in country music I've had to neglect my home and family," Loretta says bitterly. "Mooney even expects me to ask permission if I want to drive into town with the babies when I'm home. One of them told the teacher at

school that I was in Tulsa in a hospital dying of cancer and that's why I was never home. It like to broke my heart."

Instead of resentment, Mooney wants appreciation. After all, he was raised to believe it was a woman's job to bring up the kids. But he took over and did a good job and he's proud of his accomplishment. Rather than praise, however, the feedback he gets is hostility.

"It hurts me just as much as it does Loretta when she's home and the babies come to me for something instead of going to her," he says defensively. "But it's just habit with them. It's not 'cause they don't love her. They do, and they understand that if she wasn't out there working her hind-end off, they wouldn't have the nice house and the pretty clothes and all the other things they like. But I will have to say having them around has made it easier on me with Loretta gone all the time. I'd probably go crazy from loneliness without them. Raising them has been more of a pleasure than a responsibility. Maybe if I hadn't enjoyed them so much, Loretta wouldn't feel the way she does."

Jealousy is another problem they share. Mooney has the reputation of being a green-eyed monster when it comes to the inevitable show-business rumors that follow his wife, as they do every star. Yet Loretta is the one who writes vicious songs of jealousy about sending another woman to "Fist City" if she fools with her man.

"I think we've both gotten better about jealousy," Mooney says. "Used to be, I'd be out here on the farm and she'd be off on the road and I'd hear something and it would drive me crazy. It's not that I don't trust Loretta. I do. It's just that when you're so far apart, you can let your imagination get the best of you—but I made a complete fool of myself twice, and I hope that's cured me, 'cause I haven't done no checking on her since. Once I heard something, so I drove all the way to Knoxville where she was working and bribed the bellman to let me in her room. I hid in the bathroom when I heard her coming so I could see who she was with. I heard her say goodnight at the door to somebody in the band, so I hid out and waited for a guy to show up later. I stayed in the bathroom, waiting, waiting, waiting, and nobody came. By that time I was wishing I could flush myself down the commode and get out of there without being seen. Finally I had to come out and confess, and I was never so embarrassed in my life. I felt about an inch high.

"Another time she was in New York and I'd been getting these phone calls about her and some guy. So I got on a plane and went up there. I hid a tape recorder under her bed, and waited till the next morning to get it out before I let her know I was there. All I heard on the tape was her calling friends and telling them she heard I was on my way up, so not to call her. That made me all the more suspicious, so I really blew my cool and had a jealous fit. I made an ass of myself and I was sorry after, but it took her a long time to get over it. Now, when I hear things I just don't let it bother me. I know she hears things too and gets just as crazy as I do.

"But no matter what people think, I'm not a wild, run-around guy. I drink, sure. I admit that. But to tell the truth it would really be hard for me to have an affair with another woman, even if I wanted to, 'cause I love Loretta too much. Oh sure, I might have a few drinks in a bar and kid around, but when it comes to getting down to the real stuff, down to going to bed, I just don't do it. I don't like that kind of carrying on, and I'm serious about that. I'm not interested in any other woman."

Loretta hoots at Mooney's denials of infidelity, though she professes not to let what she hears bother her anymore: "Naw. He can't hurt me the way he once could," she says. "I made up my mind a long time ago that what is, is, and I'm not gonna make myself sick worrying about what he's doing when I'm not home. But if I ever *catch* him . . ." She doesn't have to finish the sentence.

Surely it is apparent by now that Loretta and Mooney do not bring out the best in one another. Both have reason to accuse. Both are wrong. Both are right. No one is really to blame, yet each needs to blame the other. When Mooney isn't around Loretta is gayer, more fun to be with, less uptight. In fact, she is careful never to appear to be having too much fun when he's around, as though she senses that any display of gaiety on her part will threaten or anger him. If they laugh together, they must do it when they are alone, because others don't see it. By the same token, Mooney is softer, less defensive, less the tough, indisputable father, more the fallible man when she's not around. And this makes him much more likable.

The little girl in Loretta still needs to please him, to make him proud (she'll never forget the sting of being sent home to mother, a failure at fourteen) while the woman in her resents the dependency role and longs for a partner. "I don't need a Daddy anymore," she says defiantly. "I'm looking for a *husband*." Yet she couldn't leave Mooney, and she knows it. "I got so mad at him a couple of years ago I told him I was going to divorce him," she says, "but we talked it out and I realized I love him. He's raised me and I'd be lost without him."

Mooney has conflicts too. He is proud of being married to Loretta Lynn, but resentful that in gaining a star he lost a wife. The adjustment to her stardom has been more difficult for him—but actually, the most difficult adjustments for both of them are just beginning. Loretta is past forty (she doesn't tell her exact age except to say, "I'm old enough to know better than to get married at 13"). She's reached the age where women begin to ask themselves serious questions, most of them more complex than the familiar "who-am-I-what-have-I-done-with-my-life" syndrome. Romantic love, sexual fulfillment, emotional adventure, intimate companionship, meaningful relationships —all of these suddenly become priority needs. An underlying fear whispers, "If I don't have these things now, tomorrow will be too late." Wrinkles appear, the body starts to sag (although Loretta is a good five years behind schedule in these areas); imagined signs of aging can be just as disturbing as real ones. Loretta says she's looking forward to old age where she can "sit back and look back on my life in peace," but the awkward middle years find her paying close attention to the laugh lines around her eyes and asking friends, "Do you think I need a face lift?" (She doesn't. Exhaustion shows in her face at times, but she is a strikingly attractive woman with cobalt blue eyes, a clear,

Loretta with her sister Crystal Gayle, who has already established her-self as a compelling singer of classic contemporary country ballads.

creamy complexion, wonderful high Indian cheekbones and a curvy little figure which she hides on stage in demure, high-necked, floor-length dresses.) Loretta is changing in more profound ways.

After spending her entire life being told what to do, how to act, what to say, she is finally becoming her own person (even her former manager, Doyle Wilburn, was dictatorial. "Now keep your mouth shut and don't show them how stupid you are," he told her when she was about to meet the Johnny Carson producers for the first time).

Dave Skepner, her manager since 1973, has witnessed her changing at close hand. "It's been like watching someone go through adolescence at thirty-nine or forty," he observes. "At thirteen, before she was allowed to develop as we know it, she was suddenly a married woman. She went from one father to another—Mooney. He's said many times that he raised her the way he wanted her. Now, in the last couple of years, she's realized there's a whole big world out there and she doesn't have to go around doing what people tell her to do all the time. Suddenly she's being allowed to express herself for the first time. And on occasion she lashes out, but it's not temperament. It's growing pains."

"She's learning daily," says Lorene Allen. "She plants those feet a little firmer all the time. She's asserting herself, saying 'It's my money, and I'll have a say in where it goes.' She doesn't always win, but at least she's putting up a fight now."

An independent wife presents a much greater threat to Mooney than a wealthy, famous one. There is no doubt that he loves Loretta and wants to make her happy, but it is difficult for him. As she changes, he becomes more and more uncertain of what it would take to make her happy. So, while she accepts their marriage (holding out no great hope that it will ever improve, yet accustomed to the familiarity of it and stubbornly determined to make the best of it), Mooney defends it, telling himself that his marriage is no worse than anybody else's. "You show me a man and woman living together as long as we've been, and if they say they don't have problems I'll show you two of the damndest liars around. There's an old saying about the course of true love never running

smooth. The only way two people could stay together and never have problems would be if they didn't care about one another and each just went their own way, 'cause when you love someone you're bound to *feel*, and it don't always feel good.

"If Loretta could be happy out of the business I know things could be good with us," he says. "When we get off by ourselves we have fun. When we went to Nassau recently, and when we went camping up in Colorado we had a great time. In Colorado Loretta was cooking and making homemade biscuits and cornbread and it was like old times. But I don't know if she'll ever be happy without singing and the people. When she slows down I want to have a lot of activities planned for us to keep her mind off it. Having the Dude Ranch on our property will help. She can always put on shows there. And she enjoys going to our place on the beach in Mexico.

"I can't say for positive but it's bound to be bearing up on her mind now," he adds. *"I've been on top so long and I can't go anywhere but down.'* She's *bound* to be thinking about that. And as she gets older the road will get harder.

"Loretta is probably one of the strongest, healthiest women alive when you think about it, because no human being could keep up her pace if they weren't strong. But it's the mental strain that wears her out physically and gets her sick. She can perform before 20,000 people and have them all love her but one, and it's *that* one she'll worry and fret over. And she's got to sign those autographs, and do those interviews and promos, 'cause if she don't she feels like she's slightin' someone. She demands too much of herself and her body fights back by gettin' sick. Then the doctor puts her on medication, and Loretta has no sense at all about medicine. She thinks if one pill is good, two is better, and first thing you know she's taking too much and getting herself all messed up. I've seen her come in off the road exhausted, with fatigue all over her face. It would hurt me so, I couldn't look at her. I'd make some excuse to leave the house and drive my truck out of sight down the road and just sit there and cry.

"But she had a real good scare last February

Loretta, who was voted one of the world's most admired women by the Gallup Poll, with some distinguished also-rans: Above, clowning in Dinah Shore's TV kitchen; left, with Charlie Rich at the CMA Awards show; below, with Gregory Peck, who looks like her father and is her very favorite movie star.

[1976]. We all did. She started to come apart right on the stage in Champagne, Illinois. Stood there with tears streaming down her face and didn't even remember it later. We put her in the hospital and took her off all her medication and got her to eating right—she was down to ninety-five pounds —and when she got out she was like a new woman. She's been a lot better since then and she hasn't been pushing herself so hard."

Loretta doesn't remember being taken to the hospital. "The first time I realized what was going on, I was laying in bed in the hospital watching TV and saw my face on the screen. They told how I was sick in the hospital and my husband was going to take me on a vacation for rest, and I thought—'so that's where I am!' I don't know if I had a nervous breakdown, but it was nerves for sure. Afterwards they put me in group therapy. I told the doctor it was really good for me 'cause listening to them, as crazy as they were, made me know I was okay."

When asked how she's changed in the past few years, this small, valiant woman answers softly. "My heart is harder."

Friends see no evidence of this. She is one of the most kind-hearted, generous stars in country music. On the road it is not uncommon for someone to approach her with an envelope containing money, repaying a loan she made months or years ago to a stranger. She has always spoken out loudly for human rights, although she is just now getting around to speaking up for her own. And she has not become thick-skinned. Today, she cares about what people think of her just as much as she did when she first walked out onto a stage.

Loretta has been phenomenally successful. She has won more country music-related awards than any other performer, male or female. She is the only woman to have captured the Country Music Association's coveted Entertainer Of The Year Award. In 1973 she made the Gallup Poll's list of the world's most admired women, an honor she considers the high point of her career. With all these accolades in her past, Mooney's suspicion that she is concerned about being on the downhill side of her peak makes some sense—but if Loretta is concerned, she is hardly distraught. "I just hope I can hang on long enough to let all the women know they don't have to take what they been taking," she says. "If all of them get together they won't have to put up with it. I'm talking about the housewives who don't have much. I'm no women's libber or nothing like that, but I know it ain't right for the women to bear the biggest burdens and have the littlest amount of fun."

As the monarch of a mini-empire—her holdings include the town of Hurricane Mills, Tenn., partnership in a talent-booking agency, a chain of clothing stores, publishing firms, etc.—Loretta is responsible for a $250,000 annual payroll, a good incentive to keep her on the road more days per year than any other woman. But that is not her primary motivation for the backbreaking schedule she maintains. The feedback from her fans and the response from her audiences hasn't diminished one bit, and as long as she can stand on a stage and feel that love flooding over her, she'll be out there singing her heart out.

"Sometimes going on stage is like walking from the dark out into the sun," she says. "It's a thrill you can't get anywhere else in life, and I guess you kinda get hooked on it. I'm my happiest when I'm out there in front of the people, singing for them. Sometimes I feel like a kid on a merry-go-round, and I don't wanna get off as long as it's still fun. Then I think to myself, 'what if you'd never had this? Would you be happy?' And I honestly believe I'd be happier. 'Course, now that I've known it, it's different. And I'm not saying I don't appreciate it, 'cause I do. But without the fans it wouldn't mean doodly-squat.

"We all know how lucky we are, even if we're not sure why God singled us out for something special. But I wonder sometimes if it wasn't just to show us what's really important. I mean, I've been a lot of places and seen a lot of things I never even knew enough to dream about as a kid, but I can tell you this: I *never* had a feeling better than holding one of my babies, and I never loved singing more than when I was rocking one to sleep with a lullaby. Everything that has happened since has made me proud and grateful, and a lot of it has been thrilling, but I never felt more important than I did then." ♥

"I don't believe in staying married any longer than you stay in love."

TAMMY

The stage lights dim as a single spotlight falls on the wistful face of a demure blonde. She sits alone on a stool, lightly stroking her guitar as she tells the audience, in a soft, whispery voice, that she is about to sing them the story of the past eight years of her life. They are quiet with anticipation, for they know they are about to hear intimate songs of a woman's search for love. Tammy Wynette is going to let them see inside her heart.

She begins the segment with "A Lovely Place to Cry," a song she wrote with George Jones in 1969, one year after they were married. It tells the story of a home, so beautiful on the outside yet sorrowful within, and the couple whose marriage has not brought them the happiness they expected.

Next she sings "Our Marriage Succeeded in Failing Today," about a couple who have every success except the one they really want, a successful marriage.

This leads into "Your Memory's Gone to Rest," a touching song about a woman walking through her empty house, taking down mementos of her ex-husband, finally laying his memory to rest.

In "The Bottle," she explains why the break-up was inevitable: " . . . but a four ounce glass of whiskey gave a better life, and a bottle by your pillow made your night."

In the closing song, "Till I Can Make It On My Own," she gives her audience a penetrating insight into her personality. She's asking the man to let her lean on him just a little while longer, until she can make it on her own. The song ends the saga of her six-and-a-half-year marriage.

Wherever Tammy performs—auditorium or night club—the audience is mesmerized during this segment of her show. When it's over, they are still so caught up in the emotion of her life that it takes them a moment or two to come back to the present and begin applauding. She has confirmed their suspicion that every single she records was either written specifically about her life, or was chosen because it could have been. She has allowed them to share the intimacy of unguarded feelings, and her willingness to suffer publicly through her music what she has already suffered privately gives her fans a feeling of closeness few singers offer the public. They leave a concert knowing

she has touched them, but more important, feeling she has allowed them to touch her. She has shared secrets and given them poignant insight into a complex personality that for all its musical exposure over the years has remained an intriguing enigma.

If Loretta Lynn is the poet laureate of the blue-collar housewife, then Tammy Wynette must go unchallenged as the heroine of heartbreak. She is the soulful *diva* for all disillusioned but undaunted romantics. No country music singer conveys emotion more poignantly. Her tearful singing style is the voice of every heartbreak a woman has ever known, her plaintive lyrics the story of every Cinderella who married her prince only to wake up in bed with a frog.

In the song with which she is most closely associated, "Stand By Your Man," she sings "If you never want to be without him, it means loving everything about him"—yet she has divorced three husbands and obtained an annulment from another.

In as lighthearted a manner as the subject will allow, she tells her audiences that her theme song should probably be one of her earliest hits, "D.I.V.O.R.C.E.," but the songs that come closest to her heart are the ones that perpetrate the most romantic illusions: "I Still Believe in Fairy Tales" (her first single after the divorce from George Jones); "I'll Keep On Falling In Love," and her particular favorite "(It Should Have Been) You and Me," the first single she released after marriage to her fourth husband, Michael Tomlin.

She sings her own life, but since she has managed to cram more trials and traumas into thirty-five short years than most people experience in seventy, her music strikes a chord in us all. Though it may have been small consolation to her at the time, every heartbreak has inspired yet another Number One hit. Her marriage to George Jones alone produced seven first place singles, prompting one disc jockey to note, "Never has one man's drinking been the inspiration for so many good songs."

Most of these songs have been written by Tammy in collaboration with her producer, Billy Sherrill, or by Sherrill alone or Sherrill and producer-writer George Richey, who is also a close friend. Sherrill, already a legend in Nashville though not yet forty, is the only producer Tammy has ever had, and she credits him with her success. "He's a genius," she says flatly.

Sherrill also discovered Tanya Tucker, and he produces or has produced George Jones, Barbara Mandrell, Johnny Paycheck, Charlie Rich, Marty Robbins, Jody Miller, Kris Kristofferson, David Houston, and dozens more, but his closest association has been with Tammy. Unlike many singers, who after stardom tend to think they know more than their producer, she relies totally on his judgement.

"If Billy told me to record 'Yankee Doodle' I'd do it," she avows, "because in the past, he's always been right. 'Stand By Your Man' is a good example. Even though I helped him write it, I wasn't sold on the song. I was married to George

Tammy, the "heroine of heartbreak," strikes some poses. In the far left photo, she tries a wistful look for a CBS album cover photo session. Near left, she delivers one of her tear-jerking solo performances. Above, again for CBS, she offers the sultry look.

at the time and he didn't particularly like it either. But I recorded it because I had faith in Billy's judgment. And it became the biggest selling country music single of all time.

"It's funny that song caused so much commotion from feminist groups when you consider we wrote it in about twenty minutes. But they took it the wrong way. I didn't sing the song to say, 'You women stay home and stay pregnant, and don't do anything to help yourselves. Be there waiting when he comes home, 'cause a woman needs a man at any cost.' No, that's not what I was saying at all," she says emphatically. "I guess I've proven that I don't believe in staying with a man you no longer love. All I wanted to say in the song was 'Be understanding. Be supportive. There'll be good times and there will be bad times, but if he's worth being with at all he's worth seeing through the bad times. Sure, he'll do things you won't like, but you'll do things he won't like, too.' And 'after all,' the line says, 'he's only a man.' "

When asked to compare Tammy with other singers he's recorded, Billy Sherrill is blunt. "She's not in a category with anybody else," he says. "She makes most of them look like jerks. She has not changed one iota since that first day she walked into my office twelve years ago to try to interest me in recording a couple of songs she'd written. She's humble and she tries harder than anyone I've ever known. She has never forgotten that the song is more important than the singer, and that's the first thing most artists forget when they become stars. They start to believe that their charisma, their talent, their magnetism will get them a hit record, and it won't. The only thing that will get a hit record is a hit song."

It hasn't been difficult for Sherrill, Richey and other top Nashville writers to come up with good songs for Tammy when she didn't write her own, because her life has provided plenty of inspiration.

Richey's idea for "You and Me" is an example. "I knew she knew she'd made a mistake in marrying Michael Tomlin although she wasn't ready to admit it, even to herself," he says. "Billy worked on the song with me and we tried to project the sentiments she couldn't express at that particular

time. It says, 'Here I am with the wrong man but all I can think of is you?' By the time the song was released she and Tomlin had split up."

The overall message of Tammy's music is the plight of the eternal romanticist looking for happiness through another human being, and coping with the inevitable heartbreak that results when love doesn't live up to its promise. The recurring theme is "all I ask is to love and be loved. All I want is to be your girl." The image is of a woman hopelessly dependent on the dictates of her heart.

Not surprisingly, all these descriptions apply to Tammy herself. But she is more complex than that, and much more interesting. She projects an intriguing aura of peasant earthiness swathed in gossamer layers of soft gentility. Both in looks and manner she exudes feminity, with long blonde hair cascading beyond her shoulders, a sensuous mouth, skin that turns honey-colored in the sun, and wide-set, warm brown eyes which are sad even when she's smiling. She is soft-spoken with a pleasant flat-land Southern drawl (as opposed to the twangier mountain accents shared by Loretta and Dolly Parton), and the voice lends credence to her ladylike demeanor. But she is also nervous, high-strung and moody. She has a healthy temper which can mushroom like an A-bomb blast, and she's not shy about showing it. She appears fragile, yet she must have been as strong as steel to have survived the melodrama of her life and channeled it into prodigious success.

In "Till I Can Make It On My Own" Tammy sings of needing to lean on someone, yet more than any woman in this book, Tammy has made it on her own. Loretta had Mooney to goad her into a singing career. Dolly Parton had her family's encouragement, and later her husband's, plus the dependable help of Porter Wagoner. June Carter Cash grew up in the business, and Tanya Tucker's father ran interference for her all the way. Tammy had no support and many obstacles, including the responsibility of three small children. Rather than encouraging her, her family questioned her sanity.

"My mother thought I was absolutely crazy," she recalls. "She wondered whether I belonged in a mental home. Here I was, a divorcee with

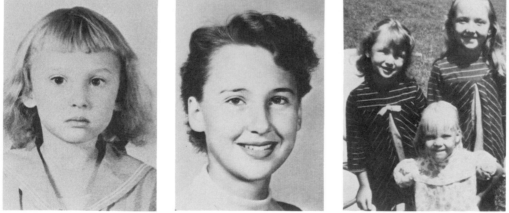

In the top photo, Tammy smiles with George Jones and the grandparents who raised her, Chester and Flora Russell. At the time Tammy was pregnant with Tamela Georgette, her and George's only child together. Above, Tammy at age five (left) and in the ninth grade (center). Above right, the three children with whom Tammy moved to Nashville, leaving her beauty parlor job in Alabama for a highly uncertain future. Left to right they are Jackie, Tina, and Gwen.

three little girls to raise, and I was leaving a steady job in Alabama as a hairdresser to go off to Nashville where I knew no one and had no work waiting for me. Looking back, I can see now that it must have seemed insane. But at the time I couldn't understand her attitude and it hurt me that she wasn't standing behind me. Since my father had been a musician, I guess I expected her to understand my need to express myself the same way. I'd grown up hearing about my father's musical talent and his desire to see me follow in his footsteps."

Virginia Wynette Pugh (Billy Sherrill chose the name Tammy Wynette) was born on May 5th on a cotton farm in Itawamba County, Mississippi, right on the Alabama line. Her father died when she was eight months old. Her mother, who was then twenty-one, went to Birmingham to get a job in an airplane factory, leaving her baby behind with her parents.

"My grandparents really raised me," Tammy says. "I called them Mama and Daddy. My mother was more like an older sister. When she came back to the farm after the war was over, she was married to Foy Lee, who was as good a step-father as anyone could want. Today he's like a real grandfather to my children. Foy and mother moved into a house across the road from my grandparents, but I stayed on where I was. I remember Foy gave me an Army cot so I could sleep in their room when I spent the night with mother, because I didn't like to sleep off by myself. So I started taking it with me back and forth between the houses. When Mama would do something to make me mad, I'd fold up my cot and drag it down to mother's house. Then when she did something I didn't like, I'd haul the cot back to Mama's. Finally, after about a year of this, my granddaddy said, 'Okay girl. Park it one place or the other.' So I parked it at his house."

From the time she was old enough to go to school, Tammy worked in the cotton fields.

"I helped plant it; I hoed it, picked it, chopped it and hated every minute of it," she laughs about it now. "I feel like Charley Pride feels. I don't *ever* want to walk through a cotton field again. Every time we pass one in the bus I get a backache."

But Tammy found a way to get out of the cotton fields at a young age. "Mama said if I'd help cook for the field hands I could work with her, so from the time I was about ten I stayed in the kitchen. I didn't mind that work at all. Even today there's nothing I like doing more than cooking a big meal."

Tammy is an exceptionally good cook and she is never more relaxed or confident than in a kitchen. She even likes housework and swears that one of the things she misses most about her present lifestyle is cleaning and scrubbing. Whereas Loretta has all but abandoned her domesticity, Tammy clings to hers as though it somehow substantiates her identity. When she is away from home she will even borrow a friend's kitchen to prepare a meal for their family. She cooks the old-fashioned way, making everything from scratch and tossing ingredients together without measuring them.

Tammy--ex-cotton-picker, ex-hairdresser--finally made it in Nashville. The large shot is one of her early publicity pictures. The small shot shows her duetting with George Jones, her idol, later her husband, and the "Mr." of "Mr. & Mrs. Country Music." Together they could squeeze tears out of a brass monkey.

Their marriage ended in divorce, but Tammy and George still like to perform together and say they have fun doing it. Here they get together at George's Possum Holler Club in Nashville for an early reunion.

When she was married to George Jones she cooked on the bus for him as they traveled between engagements. Her bass player and road manager, James Hollie, says he will never forget the picture of Tammy, full-blown in pregnancy, balancing herself precariously in the narrow aisle of the bus, cooking up cornbread or greens because George didn't want restaurant food if Tammy was around.

She enjoys "doing for a man" even under difficult conditions. As a young bride, just out of high school, she had to haul her water from the stream and make her meals on a wood-burning stove, but it didn't dim her romantic vision of the domestic life.

"In those days my dream was to own a little farm with a pretty white house and a modern kitchen," she recalls. "I wanted to do all the housework myself and I daydreamed about how I'd keep it spotless and my husband would be proud to bring his friends there."

Tammy didn't think seriously of a career in music until after her first marriage had broken up. Before that it had been a fantasy, one she never actually believed would happen.

"I always told myself it was all right to dream, but whoever heard of a Mississippi farm girl with no experience except singing in church and the high school auditorium actually making a living at it?

"Then I made up my mind to try it anyway, even if it was a daydream. But before I could do anything about it, I discovered I was pregnant. Gwen, my oldest daughter, was four. Jackie was three. My divorce was already under way, and I found out I was three-and-a-half months pregnant. I was afraid the Mississippi judge wouldn't grant the divorce, so I moved to Birmingham, 125 miles away, to live with my father's mother. I decided to enroll in beauty school because I couldn't very well start out to become a singer with a baby on the way. I thought, 'Well, if getting into country music was a ridiculous idea before, it's really out of the question now.' But the dream wouldn't die. I had no money at all. I was working for tips at the beauty college and that few dollars a week went to buy things for my girls. My father's parents and his sister and her

husband were really good to me during that time because they let me live with them and Grandma Pugh took care of Gwen and Jackie while I went to school.

"I had to wear clothes that would hide my pregnancy at beauty college 'cause they weren't supposed to accept students in that condition. And they were probably right. Standing on my feet all day may be one of the reasons Tina was born premature. She only weighed two-and-a-half pounds, and she was the most pathetic-looking little thing you ever saw. She had to be kept in an incubator for three months. I didn't get to hold her until she was a month old. Then, I no sooner got her home from the hospital than she went into convulsions and I had to rush her back. They diagnosed it as spinal meningitis, and they put me in isolation with her because the disease is so contagious.

"I sat there with her day after day praying for some sign of life. She only weighed five pounds then. Her neck was swollen out even with her shoulders and her little head was all drawn back and there were tubes going in and out of her. And she just lay there, unconscious, as still as death. I remember thinking, 'Of all times to be alone, with a critically ill baby and no husband to turn to.' I guess I never felt so alone as I did then.

"They told me if she survived she'd probably be mentally retarded. I thought, 'I don't know how I'll take it if she dies, or how I'll take care of her if she lives.' I remember praying, 'Let me get through this, Lord, and I can take anything.' I sat there for seven weeks before she regained consciousness. But four years passed before I knew for certain that my daughter was not mentally retarded."

Through her uncle, who was a technician at a Birmingham TV station, Tammy got a job singing on a local early morning show. She finished there at 8 a.m., then went to the salon where she worked all day as a beautician.

The move to Nashville in 1965 was made on sheer guts. She arrived with three children under six, no job, no contacts and very little money. And her first impression of Nashville was that it was the coldest, most inhuman place she had ever seen.

"I couldn't afford an apartment and I was turned away from boarding houses because I was a singer. They said they didn't rent to singers and musicians. They made it sound as though what I did wasn't respectable: Now that country music has become the second largest industry in Nashville, that attitude has changed considerably," she notes wryly.

She pounded the pavement of Music Row for three months before she found her way to Epic Records and Billy Sherrill's office.

"I think I was about her last hope," Billy observes with classic understatement. "She came in with some songs she was hoping to get recorded by one of my artists. They weren't bad but I was more impressed with her voice. The next day I heard a song on the radio called 'Apartment Number Nine' that I thought was good. I called the small label it was on to ask if I could lease it, and they turned me down, so I remembered Tammy and thought, 'Well, I'll just cut it with her.' I called and asked her if she wanted to do a session and she said, 'You're kidding!' The day before, nothing had been discussed about the possibility of her recording. I found an old contract in my drawer and inked out the name on it and wrote hers in. I don't know how legal it was, but it worked. We recorded the next night and everybody was knocked out over the way she sounded,

The public side of the "Mr. & Mrs. Country Music" institution: Tammy and George in a typical record company publicity shot.

so clear and precise, yet with such feeling and a piercing quality when she hit certain notes. 'Apartment No. 9' didn't go to Number One, but just about everything else has since.''

As a teenager back on the farm, Tammy's idol had been George Jones, the man known as the country music singer's singer. Billy offered to introduce her to him at the studio one night, and Tammy still remembers being "so thrilled I didn't know what to say to him."

"I was getting bookings by then, but I wasn't making any money," Tammy says. "I remember the first big job I had. I got a call from Shorty Lavender's office—he still books me today—and they said I would work in Atlanta for one week for $500. That was the most money I ever heard of in my life. What they didn't tell me was that I had to pay for my motel room, my food and hire a band. I had to do *five* shows a night for seven nights. And of course I had to pay a babysitter in Nashville while I was gone. I ended up with $90 profit for a week's work! When George and I got married in 1968 I'd had eight number one records and I was still making only $500 a night and paying a band plus all my travel expenses."

Musically speaking, Tammy and George were the match of Nashville. His soul-wrenching style proved a perfect complement to her heart-touching sound, and between the two of them they could pull a tear from the eye of a brass monkey.

A happy moment in a stormy home: ex-hairdresser Tammy plays with George while their daughter, Tamela Georgette, copies Mommy's moves.

Their haunting duets soon earned them the title "Mr. and Mrs. Country Music," and when their baby daughter, Tamala Georgette, arrived to bless the marriage, it appeared as though Tammy would at last have her happy ending.

Although she had recorded a string of hits by the time they married and won a Grammy award as well, Tammy was still a "newcomer" compared to George's super-star status. He had already become a country music great while she was still in high school, and in the beginning their relationship was an odd mixture of husband and wife, star and fan.

Although George obviously adored Tammy, she doted on him and deferred to him both on stage and at home. Even after the marriage started to go sour she still marveled at the wonder of being on the same stage with George Jones. She felt more comfortable working with him than she did alone, and her confidence as a performer depended more on his response than that of the audience.

Because she had married her idol, Tammy needed to keep her husband, her hero, on his pedestal. But George kept falling off right at her feet. She knew he had a drinking problem before they married—it was as much a part of his image as pills once were to Johnny Cash—but in typical romantic fashion Tammy thought that love would be intoxicant enough. It was for a while, but only after she had walked out, threatening divorce if he didn't give it up.

Their hit, "We're Gonna Hold On," was a result of that reconciliation, but George was soon up to his old tricks again, disappearing for days at a time on booze binges that left them both sick —him physically and her emotionally. It ended, of course, with a song. "We Loved It Away" made the charts just about the time Tammy made the divorce announcement.

Legends cast long shadows, and Tammy had been living in George's since the day they married. She worried about how the divorce would affect her career, because not only is George loved by country music fans, who identify with his suffering, but George and Tammy had been working as a team for so long that bookers had become accustomed to hiring them together. Three months' worth of bookings were cancelled immediately after the separation by places that didn't want either of them without the other.

Finally Tammy was able to line up new dates as a solo act, but months went by before she regained her confidence on stage. In the beginning she couldn't get through three songs before someone in the audience would yell out, "Where's George? When are you two going to get back together?"

The divorce did have an effect on her career, but ironically, it enhanced it. It allowed her to emerge from George's shadow to become a superstar in her own right, and it also gave George and her the opportunity of re-uniting professionally under more pleasant circumstances than those under which they worked as man and wife. As the Sonny and Cher of country music, Tammy and George represent a couple who tried to make it but failed, and yet still feel affection and respect for one another. Audience response today is more enthusiastic than ever. As Tammy points out, "George and I not only get along better now, we sing together better. The fans seem pleased that George and I have a good relationship. I explain to them that although George Jones will always be my favorite singer and a part of me will always love him, I am no longer *in* love with him and could *never* live with him again.

"I love my relationship with George now. Having never had a successful marriage, I'm at least glad I've got *one* successful divorce," she adds in a tone implying more pain than bitterness.

Tammy is as sensitive to criticism as litmus paper is to acid, and the subject of her four marriages is a touchy one. Although she does have a sense of humor about the soap opera-like script of her life (she sometimes refers to herself as "Tammy Wynette, Tammy Wynette") she does not like to be put in a position of having to explain herself. She resents the fact that the general public has the privilege of making their mistakes in private. "I guess the loss of privacy goes with the territory of being a celebrity," she observes, "but that doesn't make it any easier to see your per-

At home on Franklin Road, Nashville, in 1974, Tammy and George display their 17,500-square-foot mansion. The bottom photograph shows their patio.

Tammy on vacation with one-time boyfriend Rudy Gatlin (Steve Gatlin is on the right) at Bryce Mountain, Virginia, in 1976. This was after George's departure and before the arrival of then future, now ex-husband Michael Tomlin, Tammy's fourth husband.

sonal life splattered all over the papers."

It hurts Tammy to think strangers might judge her on the basis of marital failure rather than emotional intentions. Like Loretta, she cares deeply what people think of her and respectability is more important to her than fame. "There's no such thing as an easy divorce, no matter whose fault is was," she points out. "If you don't go into marriage lightly, and I never have, then you can't walk away from it lightly. It makes you feel sick inside and very disillusioned, and pretty soon you start wondering, 'What's wrong with me?'

"My first husband—Gwen, Jackie and Tina's father—deserted us. I didn't leave him. So in that case I really don't feel to blame. In the twelve years since we split up he has never made an attempt to see his children, never payed a dime toward their support, never even as much as sent them a Christmas or birthday card. George legally adopted them and was more of a father to them than their own father ever was.

"It was my fault my second marriage to Don Chapel didn't work because I married a man without being in love with him. But I honestly thought love would come later. I didn't know a soul in Nashville and I was living in a one-room efficiency with three children under five. His sister befriended me then introduced us, and she would offer to watch the kids while we went to a movie. I guess I married him out of loneliness. We were only together nine months and the marriage was annulled.

"As for George, it was his drinking that broke up our marriage. When we got married I *knew* we were going to be together for the rest of our lives. But it's not easy to live with an alcoholic and I simply couldn't cope with it. I tried to make it work for six years, but the emotional strain was too much. I never knew from one minute to the next if I would find him sober and sweet or drunk and mean. I used to tell him, 'George, you're gonna kill my love for you if you don't stop killing yourself,' and he'd say, 'Naw, that won't ever happen,' but it did.

"Then Michael Tomlin came into my life at a time when everything around me was falling apart. George and I had been divorced almost two years, and I had adjusted to that, but I had not adjusted to a 'dating' life. That's something I never had, even as a girl, because I married the first boy I really ever went with. When you're on the road fifteen to twenty days a month, you don't have much time to date anyway, so my social life was very limited. I was dating professional football player Tommy Neville, Len Hughes, a coach at Vanderbilt, and I had dated Burt Reynolds a few times.

"The situation with Burt Reynolds wasn't one I wanted to pursue because of the publicity involved. I can't bear to see my name in print linked with this man or that man. It goes against the grain of my upbringing somehow. And with Burt, because of his image and his stardom, the publicity was greater than with anyone else. I also didn't think it was fair to him. He's not at all like his 'sex symbol' image and every little thing he does or says is exaggerated in the press. I simply didn't want to add to that because he was very special to me.

"But I wasn't seeing him, or Tommy or Len, regularly or frequently because of my schedule and theirs. Rudy Gatlin was the one I spent the most time with, and soon I was having to defend myself about that.

"Rudy was working as a singer on my show, along with his brother Steve, his sister Donna and his brother-in-law Tim. Their older brother Larry Gatlin had brought them to me when he heard I was looking for back-up singers. They have marvelous voices and I was thrilled to have them working with me. Meanwhile I had hired Steve's wife, Cynthia, who had been a school teacher when they lived in Texas, to stay with my girls while we were on the road, so I felt close to the whole family.

"On the road, if we had a night off, Rudy and I would go to a movie, or go bowling together because we were the only two single ones on the bus. I had so much fun with him, he made me feel like a kid again. Rudy is ten years younger than I am and dating him was like getting a chance to re-live those years in my early twenties that had been very hard and unhappy for me. We began spending more and more time together and this caused big disruptions in his family because Larry was against it. I couldn't understand this and it really hurt me. I loved Larry Gatlin to death and as a songwriter I thought he hung the moon. I had been one of the first singers in Nashville to record his material, and it didn't make sense to me why he was so upset about my dating Rudy. I felt he had turned against me and I didn't know why. When you're dating somebody and working with them too, there's bound to be friction once in a while, but with Rudy and me everything always got blown out of proportion because of outside interference.

"I was living under a lot of tension anyway because of things that had been going on at my house since George and I divorced. We were getting threatening phone calls, people had broken in, we frequently heard noises outside at night, and it was terrifying. We'd had to call the police several times a month to report prowlers. They'd come and find cigarette butts on our flat roof, footprints on the grounds, a broken window, burglar alarm wires cut, the skylight opened. Once I came home and someone had come in through the skylight and written filthy words in lipstick all over my walls and mirrors. Another time when we were all out bowling, someone had broken in and turned on the kitchen faucets full force and flooded that part of the house. One night the girls and I were sitting around watching television and someone smashed in the barred window in that room, shattering glass a few feet from my daughter's head. The police never caught anyone or came up with any solution. At one point I hired guards to patrol the place at night, but during the two months they were there nothing ever happened, as though someone knew exactly what was going on at my house. It was very frightening.

"Then came the night of the fire. We'd been hearing noises outside again, and we all got scared. We were a houseful of women—my four daughters and two girlfriends of theirs, and my aunt and my grandmother Pugh, who were visiting from Alabama. I called Rudy and asked him if he would come over and stay with us until we decided if we wanted to go spend the night with my friends George and Sheila Richey.

"We were all in the kitchen the first time we smelled smoke. Rudy ran down the hall and saw it coming from under the door of the office, which is near the front of the house. Rudy got the kids outside and the fire department came and put it out. After they left, I called Sheila Richey and said we were definitely coming over, but before I could get my nightclothes packed, my daughter Jackie came running into my bedroom and said, 'Mama, I smell smoke again. There's another fire.'

"Smoke was pouring out from under the door to the trophy room, which is separated from my bedroom by a large closet. We ran outside and flames were leaping ten feet out of the house and even though it was pouring rain by then, the fire

was spreading. We couldn't understand why the fire alarm hadn't tripped, so we ran in to call the fire department and all the lines were dead. It just happened that a reporter for one of the TV stations drove by to check on the first fire report, and we used his mobile phone to call for help. It took the fire department what seemed like an eternity to get there. Meanwhile Rudy and me and the oldest girls were carrying buckets of water from the pool to try to put it out. Before it was over, the fire, water and smoke damage had destroyed three rooms and done thousands of dollars' worth of damage to four more.

"But the worst was yet to come. Between the arson squad and the insurance investigators we were all put through grilling and harassment that was totally unfair and unlike anything I could have imagined.

"Even with all the police reports on record of previous break-ins around the house, they insisted it was done by someone on the inside. We all took lie-detector tests, and as each of us was cleared they seemed more desperate to pin it on the next one.

"First they accused Rudy and they put him through hell. They even allowed an article to be printed in the Nashville paper insinuating he had done it. Then when they were forced to admit they'd made a mistake and he was cleared, they buried that news way inside in the paper where no one would notice it.

"Then they said Gwen, my oldest daughter, had done it because I had bought a house in Florida and she didn't want to move there! I said, 'That's strange logic. If she wanted to stay here, why would she burn her house down, which might force us to move to Florida?' But they put her through hours of questioning time after time, and tried to trick her into confessing. She took a lie-detector test and passed, then they accused her girlfriend of doing it! They put her through the same kind of harassment until they were satisfied she was innocent. Then they said it was my aunt! But the topper was when they accused my 85-year-old grandmother.

"Can you picture an old woman sneaking down into the basement to cut all the phone wires and the burglar alarm system, which someone had done, then going out in the rain to the bar by the pool and ripping phone wires out of the wall there, then drenching a bed with some kind of chemical—they said something highly flammable had been poured to start the second fire—then running back and hiding in her bed and pretending to be asleep, which is where we found her when the second fire broke out?

"I told them repeatedly how the fire was started but they wouldn't listen to me. We had all gone out to the movies earlier that evening and somebody got in the house while we were gone and waited until we returned to set the first fire. They were hiding when the fire department came. There are 17,500 square feet in that house and plenty of places to hide. Then they set the second fire and escaped in all the confusion.

"Seven months later the case was still open. Part of my house was still boarded off, including my bedroom, and they would not let me in there to have repairs made, nor would they settle the claim. Rain poured in because the fire had left holes in the roof and at night you could hear rats scurrying around in there. The year before my fire insurance cost me $3,000. Now it's $27,000, and now I have to pay the first $25,000 damages in case of a claim.

"The fire was the final straw. It had been a tear-down year for me. I'd had surgery three times—for a damaged kidney, for adhesions, and for cystic mastitis. I'd been hospitalized two other times for an inner ear infection and nodules on my vocal chords. They said they might have to strip them, which can be a horrifying thought for a singer. My longtime housekeeper had moved back to Florida and I worried more about the girls when I was on the road. My grandmother, the one who raised me, had died and my grandfather was in critical condition with a stroke. And I was living in a house I knew somebody could get in and out of whenever they wanted to and not get caught. This was the state of my life when I began dating Michael. The relationship with Rudy was never the same after all he was put through because of the fire and the Gatlins ended up going to work for Larry.

Tammy on a working evening backstage being clasped by fellow Columbia Records artist David Allan ("Mysterious Rhinestone Cowboy") Coe.

"I had met Michael about a year earlier through my hairdresser, Nanette Nichols, who had once dated him. He began calling me for dates and he presented himself to me very differently from what he actually was.

"He was outgoing and good-looking and he also led me to believe he was well-to-do. He was in real estate, he drove a Mercedes (which I found out later was rented . . . even the furniture in his office and his apartment was rented) and he drank Dom Perignon at $45 a bottle as though it was as cheap as Lone Star beer. He leased a Lear jet to fly to Michigan to see one of my shows (that bill came to the house after we were married) and everything he did was first class all the way. He was romantic, attentive, a take-charge kind of guy, and I was swept off my feet. I was tired of living alone, and after the fire, afraid of being alone. I thought Michael would protect me and share my responsibilities, both financially and as a parent. Not that I was after money, but I didn't want a man who was after mine, either. And I thought it would be good for the girls to have a father figure around.

"We had a beautiful ceremony on the lawn at my home, the only *real* wedding I've ever had. But I ended up paying for it. The flowers alone cost me $7200.

"When we returned from our honeymoon in Hawaii, which had also been charged because the bills were later sent to my house, I had to be taken to the hospital for emergency gall bladder surgery. While I was in there, Michael went to my bank and told them he needed to borrow $8000 to get me out. The bank manager let him have the money, then called John Lentz, my attorney, and said, 'Hey, you'd better get Tammy some more medical insurance if her bills are running that high.' John didn't know what he was talking about because there was actually no balance due on my hospital bill.

"When I got out of the hospital we flew to my house at Jupiter Beach, Florida, so I could recuperate. Michael brought another couple along, friends of his from Nashville. The first night we were there they were drinking and partying and he ended up running up and down the beach shooting off a pistol into the air. The area is very exclusive—Perry Como's house is the next one down the beach—and I didn't want any trouble with the police being called, so we had words and he took the car and his friends and left. The next morning two strangers showed up at my door and said Michael had told them they could have my house for the week. They had driven over from Nashville!

"By then I was sick with terrible pains in my stomach and running a high temperature. I told my daughter I had to get back to Nashville to the hospital because something was wrong."

But Tammy only made it as far as Atlanta. She collapsed in the airport before they could change planes for Nashville and had to be hospitalized there. A pus-pocket had formed behind her incision, and infection had spread throughout her abdomen.

By the time she was released from the Atlanta hospital and had returned to Nashville, Michael had moved out of her home. Apart from their two week honeymoon, they had actually lived together only three short weeks. Tammy asked for an annulment but Michael insisted on a divorce.

"The worst thing about the marriage to Michael was what it did to me mentally," Tammy admits. "I'm beginning to really get paranoid and bitter, and that's something I *don't* want to do. I'm beginning to lose faith in myself, and I'm hurt by the talk it's brought—'*Four* marriages? What's she trying to do—set some kind of record?'

"The fact is, I prefer married life to single life, and I would *love* to be married and *stay* married. But now I wonder if I'll ever have a happy marriage. I had heard a few things about Michael before we were married, but I shut them out because I didn't *want* to believe he was after my money. If you allow yourself to think things like that, then you become suspicious of every man you meet, and nothing is sadder than a jaded lady. I feel that if I ever let myself get like that I'll be lost."

Tammy knows, just as other women in her position know, that the more money and fame a woman acquires, the more difficult it is to find happiness with a man. And because happiness with a man is more important to her than fame and money, she finds herself in a perplexing, depressing dilemma.

"That's one of the nice things about dating Burt Reynolds," she says thoughtfully. "At least I know he doesn't want to become a singer, or want me to record some song he's written, and he sure isn't after my money. And he knows I don't want to be an actress and I don't need his money, so we can relate to one another as people, not celebrities.

"We have a close friendship, and it will last no matter who he ends up with or who I end up with. That's a nice feeling. I have my career, and I wouldn't give that up entirely for anyone. Anyone who asked me to wouldn't have my happiness at heart anyway. And he has his career, and we're both very busy, so we don't put any pressure on one another. But when we are together we have great fun because we have so much in common. We have similar backgrounds—old-fashioned Baptist upbringing—and he's very down to earth. He gets as excited over eating pinto beans and cornbread at my house as someone else might over a gourmet meal in a fancy restaurant.

"Right now my life centers around my family, my children. Gwen and Jackie are fifteen and sixteen, at ages where they are companions as well as daughters. We have good times together. And Tina and Georgette, who are twelve and six, are growing up so fast I don't want to miss any of it."

Unlike Loretta, who feels her career has cheated her of a relationship with her children, Tammy believes she is closer to her daughters because of her work. "When I come in off the road I'm so homesick to be with them that I value the time we have more than mothers who see their children every day," she explains. "We are very close

and really *enjoy* one another.

"Once, when I was married to George, one of Tina's teachers sent a note to us saying she was obviously not getting enough attention at home because she was causing disturbances in class and did not understand some of her work. It made me furious. I called and explained to her that George and I only worked ten days a month and were home more than average parents. I told her if she'd bothered to check Tina's records, she would have learned that she was a hyperactive child as a result of the meningitis, and that her behavior in class was a part of the pattern. At that time she required daily medication for her condition, but she's outgrown the need for that now.

"I absolutely will not let *anyone* make me feel guilty about being a working mother. It's a fact of life that I have to work, or none of us would eat. And the fact that my work is music is lucky for all of us. They certainly have it better than when I was a hairdresser, coming home at night dead on my feet, too tired to have fun with them, and too poor to take them anywhere. Now I come home eager to be with them, and if we want to take off a few days and go to Florida or to Colorado skiing, we can do it."

Tammy's daughters are as different in looks as they are in personality. Gwen, a brunette, is the quietest and most reserved. Jackie, a redhead, is more outgoing, the "mama" of the group, the one who makes sure everyone gets up on time to get ready for school. Tina, a cute blonde, is tomboyish and very musical (she recorded an album with George and Tammy when she was eight, and already writes songs). Georgette, a six-year-old charmer, looks like George Jones and even has some of his mannerisms.

Tammy is not a strict mother, but she really doesn't have to be because her daughters are ex-

In the top photo, the Wynette clan -- Jackie, Tamela Georgette, Gwen, and Tina (standing in front) -- poses for a family picture. Right, Tammy and "Mary Hartman, Mary Hartman" star Mary Kay Place play with Tamela Georgette at a music business party. Far right, a solo Tamela Georgette, the pride of Tammy and George's marriage.

ceptionally well-behaved and considerate of their mother's hectic schedule. "If they have a problem, they don't call me with it on the road," she says gratefully. "They know it would affect my performances. So they wait until I get home, and then we iron it out.

"Gwen dates now, but only on weekends, and she has to be in by eleven unless she calls and lets the housekeeper know where she is, and why she's late. I trust my girls, but I want to know where they are and who they're with when they're out. I'm trying to raise them to be individuals and not to be led by what the other kids are doing. I don't believe in the double standard, but I don't believe in girls being promiscuous either. We talk openly about sex, something I could never do with my mother.

"I won't raise my daughters to think boys can get away with things girls can't. I hate the kind of thinking that says 'if a girl gets in trouble, she pays, but the boy gets off scot-free because that's the way it is,' but I don't think it's right for a girl to grow up thinking she can have all the sexual freedom in the world either, because she'll end up getting hurt. I've explained to Gwen and Jackie that one man will love them more for being themselves than a half-dozen could love them for being too free. I'm glad my daughters are growing up in times when girls are taught not to be so dependent on men. I want them to be as independent as I'd like to be. But regardless of what my girls ever did, I'd stand by them.

"The one thing I would not tolerate is their being rude or inconsiderate, or if they acted like they were special because their mother is a so-called star, but they've never done that. They're proud of me, but I'm just Mama to them and that makes me proud. I want very much to be known as a good singer, but it's just as important to me to be known as a good mother.

"I know Tina and Georgette will both end up in the business, but Jackie and Gwen couldn't care less. Gwen wants to go to college in Colorado and study conservation or ecology. Jackie will probably end up being a housewife, which pleases me. She's very motherly and has a lot of patience with the younger ones. When I spank

Georgette for something, Jackie will come to me later and say, 'Oh Mama. She's just a baby.' There's a little bit of jealousy between Tina and Georgette, but that's natural. Tina was the baby for so long and we kinda spoiled her because she'd had so many problems."

Tammy is an indulgent mother when it comes to spending money, but she's equally generous with friends. She gives outrageously expensive gifts and unlike June Cash, a born bargain hunter, Tammy never checks the price of anything, whether she's buying a pair of stockings or a new automobile.

Although she meets a $20,000 a month payroll and employs more than a dozen people, Tammy plays down the "boss-lady" image, even with her band members, James Hollie, Freddy Haws, Sonny Curtis, Jim Ebert, Charlie Carter and Charlie Justice.

"I think of them as my second family, my 'road' family," she says. "They were with George before we married, then we all traveled together for six years. After the split, they decided to come with me and I was so happy because that was a difficult time for me and traveling with a group of strangers would have been really unsettling.

"I tell the boys they work *with* me, not for me. I ask their advice about things because I don't want them to ever get the idea they're just out there to back me up. They're much more important than that, both on the show and as friends.

"I have a good business head but I like to think of myself as a woman in the business rather than a business woman. The people I turn to most for advice are John Lentz, my attorney, Billy Sherrill, my producer, Shorty Lavender, my partner in the booking agency, and George Richey, who is such a good friend. I respect their opinions. I listen, then I go home and think about it for a couple of days, then in the end I do what I want to do." She laughs. "But really, that's the only way that makes sense to me. It's the only way I can live with myself. If it's wrong, then it's me. I've got only myself to blame. But at least it was *my* decision."

Tammy has obvious regrets but few guilts about her life, and none of them have to do with

Backstage at the 1976 Country Music Association Awards Show, the First Family of country music re-unites for a few moments.

the conflict between home and career. It is possible, however, that she does suffer from that widespread rural Southern malady, Protestant guilt, one symptom of which is a suspicion of and discomfort with too much worldly success.

Fifteen years ago Tammy was living in a three-room log house on a Mississippi farm with no electricity and no bathroom. Today she lives in a one-and-a-half-million-dollar mansion with twelve bedrooms, two dens, two dining rooms, a kitchen and breakfast area, a nursery wing, an enormous living room, a music room, an office, a wine cellar and fifteen bathrooms. The nine-acre grounds include a park-like playground with suitable equipment, a swimming pool, tennis courts and a guest house. The five-car garage contains a small fleet of cars, including an electric golf cart for running down to the mail box on Franklin Road. And if this isn't enough to motivate guilts, there's also a mansion on the beach in Florida (built around an indoor swimming pool with a roll-back roof) and her other 'home-away-from-home,' a $140,000, custom-designed bus. Her utility bills in the Nashville house alone run seven to eight hundred dollars per month, a far cry from the twenty-eight dollars-a-month rent she payed to live in a Birmingham government housing project in 1964.

Surely there's sin somewhere in all this, and since Southern sin does not go unpunished for long, it may well be that Tammy unconsciously seeks ways to pay for hers—destructive relationships and continual medical problems, for instance. Although they are definitely real, most of her medical problems are brought on by the fact that she never allows herself enough time to recuperate from an illness or operation before heading back to work. More often than not she has to check herself out of the hospital because doctors refuse to release her, and the next night she's on stage again. Her excuse for doing this is that she feels too guilty when she has to cancel bookings and disappoint fans, and also because time lost can never really be made up and her expenses go on whether she's working or not.

Like Loretta, Tammy is kinder to others than she is to herself. Their combined medical bill pay-ments could probably dent the national debt. Neither of them can get through a year without at least three or four trips to the hospital. Tammy has had seven serious operations in two years, and has been hospitalized at least three other times for such ailments as bronchitis and an inner-ear infection.

Friends worry about her and caution her to watch her health, but she wants their sympathy more than their scolding, and the same is true of involvements with the wrong men.

"Tammy is absolutely blind to any faults in a man when she's in love," George Richey notes, and John Lentz observes that "her romanticism is endearing, but not very practical. It usually ends up costing her money as well as anguish and pain."

But even though she can be exasperating, her friends are sympathetic. "Sometimes you want to shake her," Richey says, "but most of the time you feel protective toward her and you want to kick the guy."

Tammy brings out this same protectiveness in women, who sense her vulnerability and know that her pain, even when self-inflicted, is very real. She is not competitive with other women, and their friendship and approval is important to her. But men are more important, and the love of a good one is the most important thing of all.

In many ways Tammy is still like that little girl dragging her army cot from place to place, not content to stay for long where she isn't happy. She lives like the song she sings:

*"My door to love has opened out
more times than in:
And I'm either fool or wise enough
to open it again,
'Cause I'll never know what's beyond the
    mountain
'till I reach the other side,
So I'll just keep on fallin' in love 'till
I get it right."* *

"I can't help it," Tammy says with a slow, sad smile. "Mistakes in love don't mean love is wrong. And someday I *will* get it right. If I ever lose faith in that, then I've lost everything." ♥

*"*Til I Get It Right"* © *Tree Publishing, Inc., by R. Lane & L. Henley*

"I've gotten more pleasure out of John's career than I ever did from my own."

JUNE

Television cameras dollied back and forth across the stage at the Grand Ole Opry as June Carter Cash stood in resigned boredom, waiting on her mark for technical problems to be corrected so they could move in for a close-up of her face. When the camera was finally in position she gave the red light a mechanical smile, holding it with the resolved determination of a beauty queen whose face had begun to crack after hours of smiling down from the parade float. Suddenly, from somewhere backstage, Johnny Cash appeared, looking over the cameraman's shoulder to tease his wife:

"Smile, sugar," he implored, making a "smack-smack" kissing noise with his mouth. "C'mon, sugar, *smile*. Thaaaat's right . . . now *that's* the real thing." He petted her with words until she broke into a warm, wide smile. She was looking at her husband with such naked love in her eyes that the moment was almost too imtimate to watch.

Satisfied he had June's best smile on tape for the TV special, the cameraman dollied back, waiting for the next star to step on the mark, as Johnny took his wife's arm and led her to a corner of the vast stage. There they sat on plexiglass props, talking and laughing softly, their dark heads close together, his big farmer's hand resting gently on her knee.

Other images of June Carter flash quickly to mind: a maternal June, on the phone backstage at the Opry, her hair in giant curlers, no make-up, oblivious to the strangers milling about as she talked soothingly to a sick daughter at home; a feisty June, cautioning a journalist she'd never met before to "write a good article on Loretta Lynn and don't make fun of the way she talks or I'll call the magazine and give them a piece of my mind;" a sophisticated June, pulling up in front of the House of Cash in a nut-brown Mercedes sedan, looking like one of those women in a classy automobile ad as she stepped out in a smart tweed hat, an exquisitely tailored jacket with suede elbow patches, and English gabardine riding britches, every inch the *Town and Country* sophisticate until she opened her mouth and called out in that wonderful Appalachian twang: "Hi. Y'all come on in and make yourself at home." All these images mean something, but June's loving moment with Johnny in front of the Opry staff and half its performers leaves the most indelible picture, for she is as emotionally dependent on

her husband as Dolly is independent of hers. Yet ten years ago you couldn't have found a dozen people in Nashville to give odds that June and Johnny would be happily married a decade later.

Ten years ago Johnny Cash was a dying man, and June Carter was a desperate woman. When word filtered back from Hendersonville to the brethren down on Music Row that Johnny was out at his lake house fighting for his life and that June had moved in to help him, the general response was a knowing look, a pious "tsk tsk," and a patronizing view that even if Johnny survived, the most June could hope to get out of it was a turbulent love affair and a broken heart. But then, this was no ordinary girl singer holed up out there with that crazy Cash. This was June *Carter* of the legendary Carter family, country music's first and only royal family. Like every Southern boy of his era, Johnny Cash grew up listening to their music on an old battery-powered radio; the Carters were superstars while he was still down on his Daddy's Arkansas farm, singing to the backside of a plow mule, and it had been that way ever since 1927, when A.P. Carter, Maybelle Carter, and Sara Carter answered an ad in their local Clinch Mountain newspaper and found themselves in Bristol, Tennessee, recording the first large-scale commercial country music in history for Mr. Ralph Peer of the RCA Victor company. That recording session led directly to today's $300-million-per-year country music industry.

Although June Carter was almost grown before she realized the extent of her family's musical contribution, she was aware of her heritage from an early age. "My earliest recollection of music is sitting in front of a shiny mahogany box with a silk screen in front of it, listening to my mother and aunt and uncle singing," she recalls. "I thought they turned into fairy people sometimes, and crawled in that box to go way off to some fairyland so they could send us back songs. I had visions of it being a wonderful place.

"It was a unique family," she says. "They were thoroughbreds. That's the only way I know to put it. They were strong mountain people who had come from fine English and Irish stock. My mother's great-great-great (I'm not sure how many 'greats') grandfather was Henry Addington, the Prime Minister of England right before William Pitt. The Addington side had come from England and settled in Copper Creek Valley in Southwestern Virginia. Even as hard-working pioneers they carried with them a certain dignity that came down through the generations. I was aware of it as a child. The Carters had been in the Poor Valley area of the Clinch Mountains since the 1700's, and before that they had settled just outside Williamsburg in a place called Carter's Grove. There was a lot of poverty involved in pioneer living, but they maintained a certain haughtiness and a proud spirit that was passed on."

The Carter Family story had begun in 1915 when A.P. crossed the Clinch Mountains to marry Sara Dougherty, Maybelle's first cousin and neighbor. In 1926, A.P.'s brother Ezra made the same

Above, the original Carter Family -- Maybelle, Sara, and A.P. Together they created much of the stylistic foundation of modern country music, and with Jimmie Rodgers were its first recording stars. The Carters, descended from an English Prime Minister, are also kin to President Jimmy Carter (it was he who pointed this out to June). On the left, the Carters meet. At far left, an early Original Carter Family album.

trip, returning with Maybelle as his bride. Maybelle and Sara immediately took to entertaining their family and neighbors with songs they had sung as children. A.P. joined in, singing bass. Sara played auto-harp, Maybelle auto-harp and guitar, the latter being a relatively new instrument in the area as most mountain music was then played on the fiddle or banjo. No recognizable style had been developed on the guitar. It was used strictly as a back-up instrument, providing rhythmic strums and bass runs behind the lead of a fiddle or a singer's voice.

Maybelle Carter, June's mother, changed all that for good. She created a method of guitar playing in which the thumb picked out the melody on the bass strings while the first finger brushed the treble strings, creating chords to accompany the melody. This innovation gave the Carter Family its unique sound, but more than that, it turned the guitar into a lead instrument. It is a fact that the guitar's modern dominance over any other instrument in the field of popular music can be traced directly to this shy, dignified mountain woman and her homespun music.

After they began recording, the Carter Family's reputation soon spread all over the South and Southwest. According to anthropologist Archie Green of the University of Illinois, the Carters were the "single most influential force on American folk music for three decades, due mainly to their phonograph records which sold in the millions between 1927 and World War II."

"Music was so much a part of our homelife that my sisters Anita, Helen, and I took it for granted," June remembers. "We thought everybody had parents and relatives who played and sang. My father, Ezra Carter, played classical guitar beautifully, although he never did it professionally. Classical music was his favorite and every Sunday afternoon we'd sit around and listen to Mozart, Bach and Beethoven. We girls learned to sing the 'Hallelujah Chorus' even before we learned country music because my father wanted us to. He was every bit as influential on our lives as our mother. He was a brilliant man who was a seeker of knowledge all his life.

"When I was a little girl Daddy was a railway mail clerk, which was probably as good a job as you could get during the Depression. Eventually he became the clerk in charge on that big train, the Tennessean, that ran on the Southern Railway. I used to think he was so important because he had to wear a gun at work to protect the registered mail. Even during the roughest part of the Depression we always had food, because Daddy always had a job."

In 1938 the Carter Family went to Del Rio, Texas to broadcast transcriptions over the 500,000-watt Mexican border radio stations, the most powerful in the world. When they returned the second year, Maybelle brought her youngest child, four-year-old Anita, with her to sing duets and a few solos. "The sponsors of the broadcast, Consolidated Drugs of Chicago, liked Anita's singing," Maybelle remembers, "so when I went home for Christmas they asked me if I had any more kids who could sing. I told them I had one, Helen, but I wouldn't promise them anything about the other one—June. She was always more interested in the outdoors and playing with her cousins than she was in music. But I thought it would be wonderful to have the girls traveling and singing with me, so I went home and started to work with them. I put June on autoharp and Helen on guitar and in two weeks they'd memorized fifteen songs. So when we went back to Texas they went along and they got paid fifteen dollars apiece a week, which was big money in those days. June was about ten then."

In those days women didn't have careers. They had husbands and babies instead, and they stayed home to care for them. But Maybelle was already working professionally by the time June was born, so June grew up in a "liberated" household in the sense that her mother and father shared the responsibility of raising their daughters. If Maybelle was away "making her music," Ezra did not fume and fuss like many husbands would do even today.

"I don't think Mama ever thought of it as a *career*," June says. "To her, making music was making music, whether they were sitting around on the porch at night or giving a concert. Even their concerts were more like a parlor visit than a show. I'd give anything if we had one on film

Maybelle Carter, June's mother. As one of the original Carter Family, Maybelle created a guitar playing style which transformed the guitar from a rhythm to a lead instrument in popular music. Arthritis forced her to abandon the guitar for the autoharp in the early 1970s, and at the time this book was completed (early '77) she was in poor health. This photograph was taken in 1973, when Maybelle was still working regularly with the Carter Sisters and Johnny Cash.

the way I remember it. Old coal oil lamps lined the stage which was set with just two chairs. Mother and Aunt Sara sat and Uncle A.P. stood alone. You could hear a pin drop. A.P. told a story with every song, why it was written, where it came from. He talked with authority and the people were spellbound. They sang songs of love, Civil War songs, slave songs, songs from the coal mines and old gospel songs like 'Little Moses.'

"Daddy loved Mother's music and was very proud of her, but I guess they lived a strange kind of existence for those days because Daddy always had a place where he could go—in Florida or Virginia—to study. After we started singing, too, Mother was always with us. And Daddy would come be with us for a while. Then something would just call to him and he'd go off to bury his head in all that knowledge he was accumulating.

"When we first started singing I thought it was exciting to travel all the way to Texas, but I didn't care so much one way or the other about the music. And I didn't have the talent my sisters had, either. Anita had this gorgeous voice that could take the top of your head right off, and Helen

"Aunt Polly" in action. June created this character for herself when she first stumped the boards with the Carter Sisters; John persuaded her to make a comeback in '76.

always had perfect pitch. She could read and play classical music. Me—what I had was a lot of guts! I didn't have the voice that either of them had, but I had determination and a natural flair for comedy which I began to develop later.

"I never envied Mother, Anita or Helen their talent because my father had stressed to us from the time we were tiny that you should *never* try to be like anyone else. He used to say, 'You, as a person, are responsible for what you are. God made you something unique and very special and if you ask His help you can cultivate your gifts to the fullest.' Mother taught us to be individuals too. Even in the beginning, when we couldn't play worth a lick, she'd make us play our instruments instead of doing it for us. We sang well together, but we only started sounding better musically when Chet Atkins joined us and taught us a few more chords. Actually it was his playing that made the difference. He was like a brother to us and we all loved him dearly."

The original Carter Family stopped performing together in 1943, by which time they had

recorded over three hundred songs, many written by Maybelle. A.P. and Sara had divorced and she had remarried and wanted to move to California. Maybelle then formed her own group, the Carter Sisters, with her three daughters, and they became popular favorites on the Old Dominion Barn Dance out of station WRVA in Richmond, Virginia.

June remembers those years as the first time she ever felt any conflict between show business and her personal life.

"I was going to John Marshall High School and wanted so much to be a part of all the campus activities. I loved performing, but I also felt it set me apart from my classmates. We did a radio broadcast early in the morning before school—I can remember falling asleep in class a lot—and another one after school. Then we'd often hop in the car and run do a concert at night somewhere. Those were the years of cadet corps and high school R.O.T.C., and the biggest honor a girl could have was being asked to be a cadet corp sponsor. I wanted to be one so bad I could taste

When the Original Carter Family broke up, Maybelle formed a new group, the Carter Sisters -- herself on guitar, with June, Helen (accordion) and Anita (bass). Above and left, Grand Ole Opry publicity shots from the mid-Fifties. Right, (with June on autoharp and Helen on guitar) the Sisters backstage at the Opry in the early Sixties.

Back home in Poor Valley, Virginia, the original Carter homestead (facing page) is still standing, and A.P.'s brother Ermine (above) still works the land. In the top photo, June leads Maybelle, Sara, and Joe Carter into the finale of a Carter Family reunion in early 1977. Over three hundred Carter kinfolk showed up. On the left, Sara Carter at home in 1977.

it. But I knew I didn't have a chance. The cadets teased me too much. We had a theme song we sang on our show to the tune of 'The blue ridge mountains of Virginia, on the trail of the lonesome pine.' It went, 'We're the Carter Sisters from the mountains and we're here to sing your favorite songs.' So those cadets would line up on the school steps when they saw me coming and sing, 'We're the *corny* Carter Sisters from the mountains . . .' and I'd just about *die!*

"But lo and behold [June Carter is one of the few women in the world who could say "lo and behold" without sounding like a Southern caricature in a Carol Burnett TV skit] in my senior year the first battalion captain asked me to be their sponsor, and I was thrilled to death. Then I was afraid he'd come and see one of our concerts and change his mind. We put on quite a show—two-and-a-half hours' worth, and not all music either. Anita did acrobatics. She could sit on her head! And I played old crazy Aunt Polly, who kicked up her heels and danced like a fool. So sure enough, one night, right in the middle of my dance, I looked down and saw my captain in the audience. I sort of froze in mid-air, but there was nothing I could do but finish the dance. I was so embarrassed, but I still got to be a sponsor, so I guess he didn't think it was as awful as *I* did."

As a girl, June bubbled over with enthusiasm for life and all it had to offer. She was fiercely independent, ambitious, affectionate, and flirtatious. Grand Ole Opry veterans who remember the Carters' first days as members of the Opry (1950) also remember that June was the "character" of the group. She was "as pretty as a picture" and as gregarious as her mother was shy.

As a mature woman June has retained many of those characteristics, but she is not so independent now, and religion plays a more important role in her life than it did in the past.

"The big change in me came about because Dr. Nat Winston told me I *had* to change if I wanted to see John get off drugs once and for all," she says. "We had found him at his house, half frozen to a tree at the edge of the lake where he's been hanging on for dear life for Lord knows how long after running his tractor into the water.

He was half-dead from pills and exposure—he had ice in his hair and his face was blue, it was freezing cold—and when I saw him I cried, 'This is it. I can't take any more.'

"I had gone through so much over John already. Even before I loved him, I couldn't stand by and watch him kill himself. I had fought him and his pills for five years, fought him in ways that were completely against my nature. I was with his show for months before I even knew he was on pills. Then I told myself it was none of my business—I wasn't emotionally involved with him—but when you work with someone they become like family and I couldn't help worrying about him. Marshall Grant (of the Tennessee Three) and I would swipe the key to John's room and sneak into his things looking for pills. When we found them we'd flush them down the commode. Then I'd face him defiantly with what I'd done. It's against my nature to fight. I had never raised my voice to a man before in my life, but I yelled plenty at John. There were times I could see in his eyes he wanted to hit me, but he'd just storm out and go look for more pills. You never knew what to expect from him in those days—he could be mean and wild one minute, kind and sweet the next. But it's funny, the basic goodness in him was always there."

One friend from that period says Johnny took things from June he wouldn't have taken from anyone else " . . . partly, I think, because he was already falling in love with her, even if he didn't know it, and partly because he had so much respect for Maybelle, who had also joined his show."

Maybelle and Johnny became very close then. Johnny was still married to his first wife, Vivian, who lived in California with his children, but their relationship was not good due to factors like his pill addiction and her (understandable) lack of enthusiasm for show business, so he fell into the habit of "crashing" in Nashville at Maybelle and Ezra's house. Despite the fact that he often broke into the house when there was no one at home to open the door, they never chastized him. Ezra read the Bible to him and prayed. Maybelle cooked for him, washed his clothes and nursed him through his pill binges. He would leave their

A young, strung, and hungry Johnny Cash in 1963, before his eventual crash and salvation by June.

house "clean" only to get blind-stoned again within a few days.

June, who was married to her second husband at that time, stayed away from Johnny when they were off the road, but she knew what her parents were going through for him. "Mother finally just kept a bed made for John at her house because they never knew when he would show up," she says. "His own parents were living in California then, but even if they'd been in Nashville it would have been too hard for him to go to them, and too painful for them to take it. Sometimes it's easier if it's not your own child. I know for sure if I had ever gotten myself in the shape John Cash was in, my father would have given me a good whipping and kicked me out."

Johnny was often too stoned to perform, and began to miss shows, which resulted in bookers becoming afraid to sign him. Nothing frustrated or angered June, the dependable professional, more than this, although she tried to cover for him, making excuses and promises she couldn't keep, not knowing from one performance to the next what condition her "boss" would be in, or even if he would be there at all. It must have been a time of unrelenting mental and emotional conflict for this woman who had been raised in a Christian home of high moral standards, who had never personally known the temptation of alcohol or pills ("I never could drink, and taking a pill to feel good would have never occured to me"), who has a demanding conscience and who, though married, found herself falling in love with a drug addict who appeared hell-bent on killing himself.

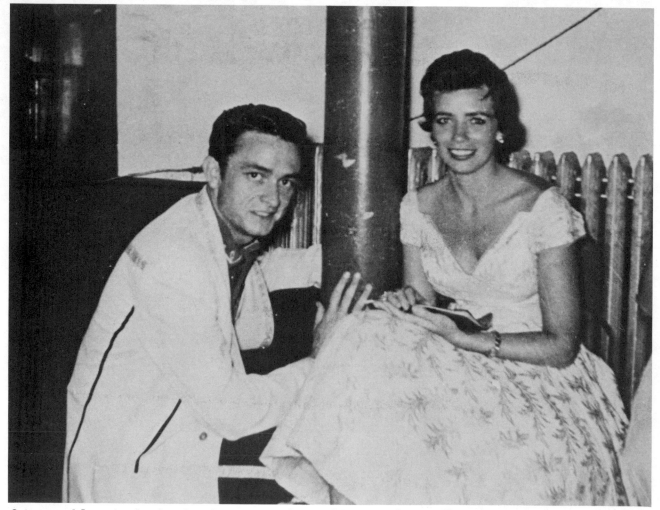

Johnny and June shortly after their first meeting. June had become a Johnny Cash fan courtesy of Elvis Presley, who used to punch up John's songs on juke boxes while he and June were working the road together.

Torn constantly between obligatory Puritan guilt over loving the "wrong" man and the Christian ethic of being "thy brother's keeper," it's a wonder she didn't end up in Parkview (the Nashville sanitorium about which Johnny later wrote a song).

But for all her Southern gentility and soft demeanor, June Carter is a strong, indomitable woman—and in the end, she did exactly what she had to do.

"When I finally admitted to myself that I cared for John, it was a terrible time for me," June recalls. "Here I was in love with this man who was on drugs, and I had two beautiful daughters, and he was so strange and unpredictable that I didn't even want him at my house around my children. My second marriage was over and I was too ashamed of that to tell anybody. I felt like a complete failure. Months went by after the divorce before I even told the people who traveled with John's show. And he was getting worse and worse. Mother had even been to Dr. Nat Winston—who was State Commissioner of Mental Health, but also a family friend—and said, 'You've got to help him. He's dying.' After Nat met John he gave him a *three million* to one chance of kicking it, because he was taking over a hundred pills a day and had been for a long time.

"So that day when Nat came out to John's house, I told him I was through. I just couldn't take anymore. Nat talked to John for a long time, then he came out to me and said, 'June, I don't know why, but I have a feeling he can kick it this time. He's reached the bottom and he knows it, and I think he's ready to straighten out. But if he's going to make it, you'll have to stay here and help him through it because the withdrawal will be severe.'

"I told him I *couldn't* move in there with John. I said, 'Nat, I'm not that kind of a girl. I can't come out here and stay with him, no matter how much I care,' and he said, 'Well, if you want him to live you're gonna have to, 'cause otherwise he's a dead man.'

"I said, 'Oh, my dear God. What can I do?' I'd been taught to live a certain way and I had never been emotionally involved with anybody I wasn't married to. . . . I mean, I hadn't had an affair, so to speak, with anybody who wasn't my husband. And I had my children to think about, and I just didn't see how I could do what Nat was asking. I remember getting in the car to drive home, crying so hard I could barely see the road. When I got home my father was sitting on the porch and I stopped the car in the driveway and sat there, too distraught to get out. Daddy walked off the porch—I'll never forget he had on this little cap he liked to wear with his overalls—and he said, 'June, honey, what's the matter?'

"I started bawling, and telling him I didn't know what to do. I said, 'John is in real bad shape and Nat Winston says I have to go and stay with him to get him through this withdrawal.'

"Daddy pulled me out of the car and looked me right in the eye and said, 'Girl what are you *waiting* on?'

"I said, 'Daddy, you know I can't move in over there with John. What about the girls? And what will the neighbors say?'

"He said, 'You don't worry about the girls. We can take care of them. And the neighbors aren't gonna say a thing because *I'm* going with you. Your mother and I will take turns being with you and we'll sleep in shifts if we have to. We aren't going to let John down now. You've got to remember the Lord has got His hand on that boy, and you're not giving up on him.'

"He marched me inside, pulled my suitcase down and packed it for me. Here was my father, who was a lot more Puritanical than I was, urging me to move in with this man who was hooked on pills. That just shows how much faith my daddy had in the Lord's plan for John Cash.

"John doesn't remember much about that first week after I moved in, but the rest of us will never forget it. If people who are tempted to take pills ever saw the agony a person goes through in withdrawal, they'd lose the urge quick.

"When it looked like John was gonna pull through, Nat Winston said to me, 'June, if this thing is going to work and you expect him to stay off pills, you're gonna have to do some adjusting too. You're gonna have to give up some of your independent ways if you truly love this man.

You've got to let him be *it* in your life. You will have to be there when he stumbles, 'cause he *will* stump his toe now and then. He's only human. When he does, if you show that independence and flare up and run off and leave him, then he won't make it. He's got to have an anchor, and that's what you've got to be.'

"So I had to make a decision. I prayed and I weighed both sides. I had my daughters and we had our home and I had a little money put away and I didn't owe anybody a dime. I knew I could earn fifty to seventy-five thousand a year whenever I wanted to, and that gave me a sense of security and independence a lot of women don't have if they're financially dependent on a man. I thought, 'Well, what's more important? Your independence or John?' and of course I knew the answer. So I said to myself, 'Well, if it goes, it'll just all go. But I love this man, and I have to see it through.'"

June and Johnny didn't talk about getting married until several months after his withdrawal period. "Johnny and I both had long, bumpy marital roads behind us," June says, "and even though we felt we were meant to be together, the idea of another marriage was kind of frightening. Two divorces can make a woman terribly unsure of herself. My first husband, Carl Smith, was a big star when I married him, and I remember telling my mother, 'I won't be working any more 'cause one performer in the family is enough.'

"When we split up I didn't know how I could stand it, or really what had gone wrong. Then after a *second* divorce, well, I just didn't know if I could ever find happiness in marriage. I was disappointed in myself and what I'd done with my life and I didn't want my daughters, Carlene and Rosey, to go through another break-up, but as it turned out it was my girls who planned our marriage. They had gotten to know John by then. At Christmas his four daughters, Kathleen, Cindy, Tara and Roseann, had come from California and my girls and I had gone out to his house for the holidays and they all got along so well. So we had started talking about getting married in June when school was out. My girls and I lived closer into town and I didn't want to change them to a Hen-

dersonville school in the middle of the year.

"I remember it was on a Tuesday in the last week of February when I decided to tell Rosey and Carlene that John and I were thinking about getting married. We were sitting in the kitchen at our house and I said, 'I love this man very much and want to marry him, but if you don't love him or don't feel you can make him a part of your life, then I can't do it.'

"They said, 'Mama, we *love* John and if you want to marry him that's fine with us, but why do you want to wait 'till June? That's so far away.'

"I explained about school and they understood. But the next day Carlene came home from school and said, 'Mama, I've got it all figured out. John can go to Franklin, Kentucky, tomorrow and get the license (there's no waiting there) and if you got married on Friday you could have a honeymoon over the weekend. We could stay with Aunt Helen. Then you could pick us up on Sunday night and we could start school in Hendersonville on Monday.' And do you know, that's exactly what we did!"

The marriage took place in 1968, and most Music City observers didn't give it much of a chance. Johnny's reputation, whether earned or fabricated, was that of a man who liked women as much as he liked feeling good on pills and roaring with the guys. And he had done a lot of the latter. There are hotel and motel managers around this country who still cringe at the name of Johnny Cash, and with good reason. He used to get a big kick out of sawing the legs off their furniture and propping it back just *so* until the next tenant sat on a bed or a chair and went crashing to the floor, or painting the walls of his room black, or unleashing a thousand baby chicks in his room before checking out. (For a long time after their marriage June kept a "couth" book for Johnny, writing down such reminders as, 'Do not sing bluegrass songs walking through airports;' 'Do not eat sardines and crackers on planes.')

The marriage, of course, did last, but the talk continued. Today, for instance, some people say that June's strong religious ties are motivated by the belief that her example will help keep Mr. Cash in line.

June with her two daughters from her marriage to Carl Smith, Rosey (left) and Carlene; they both offered full approval of their mother's marriage to Johnny Cash.

Chet Atkins, who has known June more than half her life, says that this is not true; that she has always been religious. "She never let it stand in the way of having a good time, but her religious roots were always deep," he recalls. "She believed strongly in prayer and thought everybody ought to use it. She was always quoting the Bible about something."

There are others who say June sometimes takes herself too seriously as Mrs. Johnny Cash, and tends to put on airs she never had before, but it's difficult to imagine anyone taking themselves less seriously than June is when playing crazy Aunt Polly on national television, or putting on fewer "airs" than she does when she spends a day on her hands and knees at the House of Cash cleaning out a storage room, or scrubbing down walls and re-painting rooms at their Bon Aqua farm an hour west of Nashville. June's critics—and they are few —are in all probability the same people who have never quite forgiven Johnny Cash for becoming a living legend instead of a dead one ("Everybody said they were proud when I pulled through and straightened up," Johnny says doubtfully. "But there are a few who haven't gotten over it yet. They had me dead, buried and in Hillbilly Heaven where they could write songs about me.").

Johnny is alive and sassy, his career is bigger than ever (he earns several million dollars a year), and he's still in love with the woman he married. They have a six-year-old son whom he adores and he has gained a whole new following among young people who see him both as a father figure of honesty and integrity and a peer who's been to the depths and survived. Johnny manages to flirt with the world of Rolls Royces, V.I.P. airport lounges, Hollywood movies and television, four-star gourmet restaurants and First Class service everywhere without being trapped by any of it or losing touch with the basics. Dinner with a Governor or a President (Jimmy Carter is related to June, and *he's* the one who contacted *them* to point it out) is not unusual, but Johnny still communicates more comfortably with convicts. "It may be hard for some people to believe," June says, "but our best times are still walking through the woods around the lake house, or fishing, or spending a weekend out on the farm, fooling around and just enjoying God's earth."

You can look at Johnny Cash's face and tell where he's been, but the scars of June's past trials and tribulations don't show on the surface. If anything, she is more beautiful in middle age than she was as a girl. Her thick chestnut hair falls softly over her shoulders. Her soft blue eyes fairly sparkle when she talks. Her voice, though "whiney" at times, has a breathy, sensual quality vaguely reminiscent of Marilyn Monroe's. She is petite—five-foot-two and 120 pounds—with a voluptuous bosom (her own), a small waistline and firm thighs. She has laugh lines, but no wrinkles, and although she's three years older than Johnny, she appears ten years younger.

Like Loretta, Dolly, Tammy and Tanya, June is oddly out of place as a millionaire. Two Rolls Royces are parked in her driveway, but they are stored there under tarpaulins like forgotten toys to make room in the garage for her overflow of antique furniture. She has a household staff of four, yet she cooks and cleans and shops for bargains and waits for sales as earnestly as any blue-collar housewife. "I'm just as stingy as I can be," she brags.

Her one extravagance appears to be antique furniture, and she has enough of it crammed into their stone and timber house on Old Hickory Lake to fill a museum. Antique lovers would consider the hundreds of thousands of dollars' worth of furniture she owns an investment, since she *does* know what is good and what is junk, but even a compulsive collector would balk at her apparent inability to control her buying. The result is that Johnny's "nature house," the rugged structure he bought as a bachelor and in which he lived and almost died before it was furnished, has become so overburdened with massive Baroque, Rococo, Gothic, Romanesque and Renaissance pieces that one expects to see Hamlet's ghost pop out any minute from behind a thirty-foot Jacobean cabinet. Even the downstairs panoramic view of the lake has been almost cut off by huge, ornately carved cabinets and cupboards.

Two more upper levels have been added to the house since they married, but June talks wistfully

Johnny Cash's "nature house" on Old Hickory Lake near Hendersonville, Tennessee, where John and Waylon Jennings used to fall out of boats. This is the house John bought shortly before he kicked his drug habit, and where June and the Carters pulled him through. Rugged and massive, it occupies a prime spot on "star land" and is home for the Cash clan.

Inside the "nature house" is June's furniture collection, seen here in part. Furniture is June's one extravagance, and it is extreme.

of the need for more space. The master bedroom, an enormous room probably as large as the entire Arkansas cabin in which Johnny was born, contains *two* huge antique beds, not because the Cashes sleep separately, but because June likes them both so much she can't bear to make a decision and part with one. Their son, John Carter, must have a half dozen antique cradles, cribs and baby beds in his two bedrooms, and they will undoubtedly be on display long after he's grown and moved to a home of his own.

June escorts a visitor through these high-ceilinged, over-furnished rooms with a mixture of pride and embarrassment. She's well aware that the decor smacks of over-indulgence and she continually apologizes—"I know there's too much in here; I know how cluttered it looks"—but in the next breath she's pointing out some interesting and historic piece with the appreciation and respect of a museum curator. She has the problem with furniture that we most often associate with food: a gourmet's taste and a truckdriver's appetite. Johnny, a huge man who fills doorways and would appear to need space in which to maneuver his large body, allows June her indulgence with the benign tolerance of a man who has never quite learned the trick of saying "no" to the woman he loves.

Outside the five-level hillside mansion, their vast lakefront acreage boasts a swimming pool, a tennis court and June's rose garden, where she often goes alone to pray and meditate. From here she can see the tour buses that pull up to her gate every half hour, allowing fans to rush out and hang over the fence, clicking Instamatics furiously, although the most they usually see is the garage side of the house and one edge of the swimming pool.

"I used to hate those buses," June muses. "But when our son John Carter was in the accident when he was four it was a tour bus that stopped and pulled the jeep off him that was crushing him. Now every time I see one I say, 'Praise the Lord! Come on, buses!' There's a reason for everything."

The accident happened when Reba Hancock, Johnny's sister, was driving a group of Cash children into town in the family jeep. The jeep skidded up an embankment, causing it to flip over, spilling children everywhere. Johnny and June were at their farm out from town when they heard that there had been an accident, and John Carter had been taken to the hospital.

"The drive in to Madison Hospital was an *eternity*," June remembers, her voice breaking even now when she talks about it. "When we got to the hospital our friends—Roy Orbison and his wife and Kris [Kristofferson], Larry Gatlin and Vince Matthews—were already there waiting. They'd heard the news on the radio. Then when they told us they had sent John Carter on to Vanderbilt Hospital in an ambulance, I fell to pieces. I thought, 'Oh God *no*. Anything but John Carter.' We had prayed so hard for a baby but I didn't think we were going to be able to have one. Then when I got pregnant, I prayed for a boy. But with six girls between us I didn't much see how John and I had a chance of getting a boy. Then God gave us this perfect little red-headed son, and it was like a gift right from Heaven. I guess the proudest moment of my life was when John came into the room after the baby was born and told me I'd given him a son. I'd been put to sleep for the actual delivery, so I didn't know what we'd had until I came to.

"When John Carter was an infant I could find John in his room day or night just looking down at him in his crib. He acted like the first man alive to sire a son. I've often thought that no matter what ever happened between John and me, I know I have something for him no other woman could ever have—I'm John Carter's mother.

"So that day when we were told he'd been rushed on to Vanderbilt, I immediately thought the worst. That drive was even longer than the first one, and I felt like my heart would stop before we could ever get there. They had to help me out of the car. I was actually too weak to walk. My legs just wouldn't carry me inside to hear the news.

"But when we got in the door of the emergency room the first thing I heard was John Carter crying! It was the most blessed sound I've ever heard on this earth. The doctor came out and said, 'As

June a few days after the birth of John Carter Cash, the only son among John's children or her own.

you can hear, he's conscious now, and it's not near as serious as we first thought. He's got a concussion, but he'll be fine.' I collapsed with joy. That's been almost three years ago, and I still can't think about it without feeling weak.

"I'm afraid it's made both John and me over-solicitious about John Carter. A few weeks ago he had a cold and I had gone down to the farm for a couple of days to work because we're re-doing some of the rooms. John called me and told me John Carter was running a little temperature, but not to worry, he was watching him and everything was fine. So I went about my work, knowing as a mother does that a little fever in a child is nothing to get upset about. But when I got home the next day I found John in a real pout. He said, 'I thought you'd come on home the minute you heard John Carter had a fever.' I said, 'But honey, you told me not to. You said he was all right.' John said, 'I know I did, but I thought you'd come on home anyway.' " June smiles maternally. "Sometimes I think John is my biggest baby of all." ' (Astrologers would say that June possesses more than her share of maternal instincts because she was born with her sun in the sign of Cancer, the most "maternal" sign of the Zodiac, but whatever the reason, she mothers everyone—Kris Kristofferson come to sit at Johnny's feet, office employees, friends, relatives, Nashville musicians. She calls them all her "babies" and fusses over them like a mother hen.)

Although June literally grew up in show business, she now leads a more domestic life than any of the other women in this book. A part of that might be due to Maybelle's influence, because even though she was an entertainer before June was born, she was always the wife and mother first, the musician second. "When Mother invited you for supper, *she* cooked, not the help," June's sister Helen recalls. "The wheat thrashers used to love to eat at our house. Mother was a wonderful cook and she loved doing for her family. When a play was given at school, a Carter girl always got a part because Mama was the best seamstress around."

June and Johnny are on the road far less than

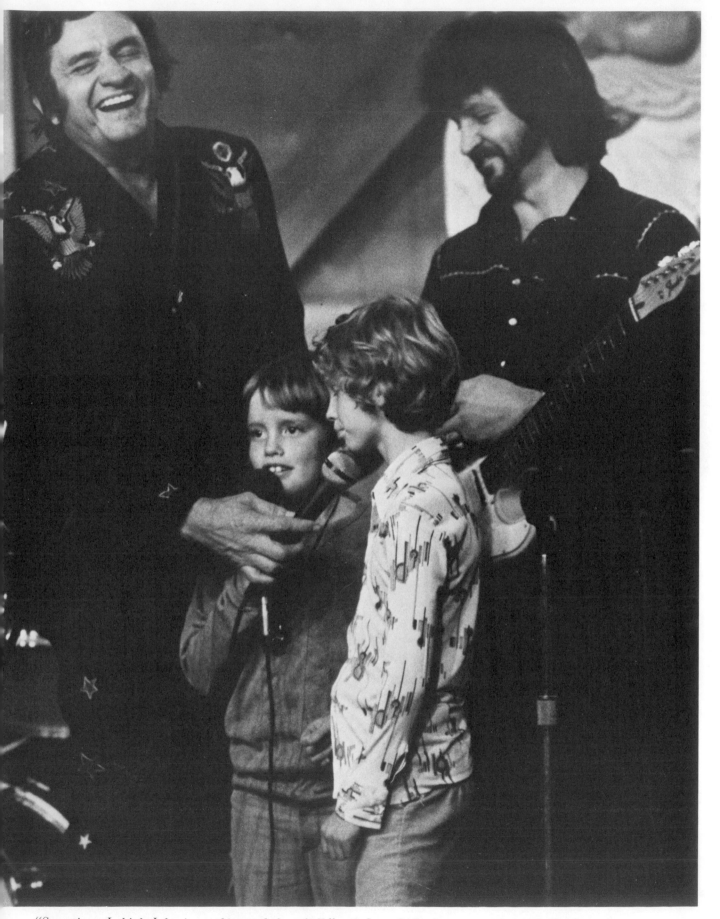

"Sometimes I think John is my biggest baby of all," says June. Left, she poses with his portrait's reflection in one of her countless mirrors. Above, he shows off John Carter (full face, holding his own microphone) to the Carter kinfolk.

Loretta, Dolly, Tammy and Tanya, who do over two hundred concerts a year. Johnny makes more ($25,000 and up) per show than, say, Loretta or Dolly, so he can work less without sacrificing any income. He and June made a decision when John Carter started school that they would allow their work to interfere with his education as seldom as possible, because they do not like to leave town unless their son is free to go with them. This of course gives June more time to be a housewife.

Maybelle grew up in an era where a woman's role was homemaker, wife and mother, with the alternative of spinsterhood about the only other option; June lives in a time when a woman has choices. Yet her domesticity, motivated primarily by how she views herself and her role as a woman, is just as deeply ingrained as her mother's. That has not always been true, but her experiences, as an ambitious "career woman" were disappointing enough to send her running toward the emotional security of husband and family.

"I've found more happiness through John's career than I ever did through my own," she explains. "I used to be *very* ambitious. Back in the fifties, before they were doing network television from Nashville, I was traveling to New York and California to do shows like Gary Moore, Jackie Gleason, Tennessee Ernie Ford and *Gunsmoke*. I had studied acting in New York with Sandy Meisner. Elia Kazan had seen me on a Carter Family show in Florida and urged me to study at his school. So I left our show and went to New York. Kazan had just made *Baby Doll* and

he was preparing *Wild River*. He wanted to do it with unknowns and he offered me the lead. But as it turned out, the producers wouldn't put up the money without a 'name,' so Lee Remick got the part I was supposed to play.

"I was doing a lot of work with Elvis at that time, too. Col. Tom Parker was handling me. I was with him when he was on *Louisiana Hayride*, and when he made his first screen test, and I did comedy to open his concert show. In fact, it was through Elvis that I first heard of Johnny Cash. Elvis loved John's records—'Folsom Prison Blues,' 'Cry, Cry, Cry' and 'Hey Porter.' That was his favorite. Everyplace we went, he'd drag me into cafes and honky tonks looking for Johnny Cash records on the juke box. I ate every meal to Johnny's songs. So when I came home to do the Opry and this tall guy walked up to me backstage, kinda shy, and said, 'You're June Carter. I'd like to meet you. I'm Johnny Cash,' I said, 'Well, thanks to Elvis I've become a fan of yours,' and he was real pleased.

"Anyway, I was proud of my career at that time but I wasn't a happy person. I was married to Carl Smith, but I wanted more than marriage. When you're eaten up with ambition you're never satisfied. I've seen it happen to so many people in this business. So when I decided to make my life with John, I made up my mind to give as much as I had, to put our life together above things like ambition and career. I knew how much I needed John and I remembered the nights when I'd been in bed alone, crying myself to sleep out of loneli-

New and happy parents. June provided John with the apple of his eye; "I have something over John that no other woman could have," she says. "I am John Carter's mother."

ness. A woman is nothing if she doesn't have a man she can love and respect."

Priorities differ, but June doesn't believe people can find happiness until their own priorities are in order: "For me, it has to be God first, John second, my children and my family next. Once I had established that, everything fell into place and I got what I wanted anyway.

"I like my career now more than ever because it's a *sharing* thing. It's something I *share* with John, or—I should say—he shares with me. He knows I like to perform, and thank goodness he likes to have me doing it with him. But there would never be any question of me going off and working by myself as I once did. Our daughters work with us, my family works with us, even John Carter gets up and sings when he feels like it, so it really becomes a *family* event. I just love that. It makes me so proud. This sounds silly, I know, but sometimes when we're all on stage together I look around me and I'm so filled with love and happiness it's all I can do to keep from crying."

June is a romantic, but she is no fool. She believes in her marriage, and in her husband, but she doesn't take either of them for granted. Someone who's known her for many years remarked that she'll "always be afraid of losing Johnny because she already lost one star—Carl Smith—to another woman, and you don't get over something like that." But millions of wives who've never been married to a star, or lost a husband to another woman, fear the same thing. When you're in love, that often goes with the territory. June doesn't try to hide this insecurity from Johnny. In fact, they talk about it openly.

"Johnny and I are both aware of the pitfalls, the temptations that can hurt a marriage," says June. "Entertainers face more than most, because they get more attention from the opposite sex than most people. I'm not one of those women who can share the man I love. It would be like cutting off my arm to share John. And he'd feel the same about sharing me. But John's human and I'm human, so we think it's only wise to guard and protect the happiness we have. And we're open about it. If we're driving along and John sees a pretty girl, I say, 'Look, honey . . . see it all.' But he knows it stops there.

"John wouldn't think of hiring a secretary, for example, without me passing on her too. He fooled me when he hired the last one, though," she laughs. "I don't think Irene would mind me telling this. We'd been looking for a secretary for John at the House of Cash, and one day he called me from the office and said, 'Guess what, honey? I just hired the perfect secretary.' I thought, 'Well, that's not like John to do that without even *discussing* it first.' I said, 'Well, what's she like?' and he knew by my tone I wasn't too pleased. He started naming off her qualifications and she *did* sound perfect, and I thought, 'Well, you'd better be careful what you say, June.' Then he got all through and he said, 'And by the way, you're gonna love her. She weighs over two hundred pounds!' "

John says that on his wedding night he prayed he would never bring June the heartache he'd given his first wife, and that if he felt tempted to slip—whether it be with women or pills—he'd remember to pray. He has slipped with pills several times since he first kicked the habit in 1967, but both he and June half expected that. "It was good that it happened," he says. "I had to keep re-learning my lesson that I can't mess with it or I'm dead. I took pills in the old days because they made me feel good, and there are still times when I'd like that good feeling, but I can't handle it and I know that. I know that for me it's a matter of life and death. I stay away from everything— whiskey too, though I never liked the taste of it and June didn't either. We don't even serve liquor when we have a party here, but nobody seems to mind. We have just as much fun without it. Other women are not a temptation because I don't have any desire to fool around. I'm happy with my marriage, with my love life. I'm deeply in love with my wife and I don't see that changing."

Virginia Woolf observed that "women have served all these centuries as looking-glasses possessing the magical and delicious power of reflecting the figure of a man at twice it's natural size," but even more magical than that is the fact that, as often as not, the man grows to fit the reflection he sees in his woman's eyes. Johnny Cash has done that, and June Carter reaps the rewards. ♥

"I am a brave little soldier. I may not
win the war but I sure fight like it."

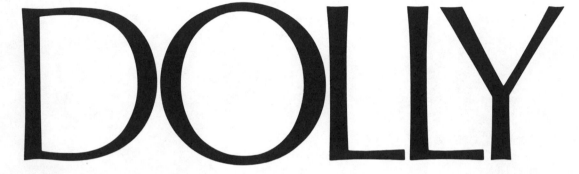

The country music industry suffers from a peculiar paranoia. With its widening acceptability, its new respectability as a valid American art form, and its unprecedented commercial success, country music still suffers from the years of humiliation and ridicule heaped upon it by practitioners of other forms of popular music. Old-timers have not forgotten the days when their music was considered the bastard stepchild of the broader music industry—tasteless "white trash" stuff which appealed to only the lowest class of Southerner—so that even now, when the stigma has faded, the resentments remain.

Any country music performer who sets out to join forces with "the enemy" is considered a traitor by most, and so the process of "going pop" (that is, selling records to a pop, as opposed to country, audience) is fraught with strife and unpleasantness. Country purists argue that if country artists abandon "traditional" sounds for something slicker, they will sacrifice their heritage to the forces of progress (with the implication that the music's pure forms will simply wither away); others in the industry simply feel abandoned, or jealous, or both.

With this climate hanging over the industry, it was no surprise that Dolly Parton, one of country's most popular performers and respected songwriters, became the target of heavy criticism when word spread that she was "going pop." Dolly had been awarded the Country Music Association's Female Vocalist of the Year Award for the second consecutive year, and had been nominated for the Entertainer of the Year Award, the CMA's highest honor, so she was in a highly visible, and controversial, position. For months, from the late Summer of '76 to the Spring of '77, there were few industry gatherings where the talk didn't get around to Dolly. The gist of the conversation was repeated over and over: "Have you heard about Dolly? She's leaving country. She's going pop. She's dumped all her old associates. Even her old friends don't hear from her. She thinks she's outgrown us."

Judging by Dolly's actions and the mystery that surrounded her career during that period, the rumors appeared to be true. Between 1975, when she won her first CMA Female Vocalist of the Year Award and 1976, when she picked up her second, she had

cut the last tie with her mentor Porter Wagoner by dropping him as her record producer; she had fired her road band, most of whom were relatives, and put together a new group of musicians who came from pop backgrounds; she had dumped Don Warden, the manager Porter had recommended to guide her career, hiring a high-powered Hollywood management firm, Katz, Gallin and Cleary, who boast such clients as Mac Davis, Olivia Newton-John, Cher, Donny and Marie Osmond and Tony Orlando and Dawn; and she had severed her eight-year association with the Nashville booking agency, Top Billing, Inc., to join a California-based company, Monterey Peninsula Artists, who book such un-country acts as Carole King, Cheech & Chong, Chicago, and the Eagles. The agency had been recommended by her friend, Emmylou Harris. Dolly had taken to hanging out with Hollywood country-rock types such as Emmylou and Linda Ronstadt. These were the facts which lent credence to the gossip that she thought she had outgrown her Nashville pals.

In the Spring of 1976, Dolly became the first female country singer to get her own syndicated television show. It was produced by Nashville's oldest television production company, Show Biz, Inc., headed by Bill Graham, who has been producing Porter Wagoner's show for sixteen years. Dolly's show appeared in 130 markets and was due to pick up more for the second season when she told associates she would not continue taping beyond the originally contracted twenty-six seg-

ments because she felt the production was not up to the standards she had anticipated. Along Music Row it was said that this was but another indication of Dolly's new attitude that she was "too good" for the local scene. (There were others, however, such as RCA's Chet Atkins, who agreed completely with Dolly's evaluation of her show.) In June of that year Dolly announced she was taking four months off the road on doctor's orders due to exhaustion and throat problems. Since Dolly is one of the very few women on the road in country music who does not seem to suffer physically from the rugged schedule, who brags that she has never had a nervous breakdown, never needs drugs or alcohol to keep her going, and has never been hospitalized for exhaustion and never will, this announcement was highly suspect. Her critics wanted to know if it wasn't just her way of getting out of bookings on the country circuit while she revamped her career and re-organized her forces. When it was learned that during this period she had gone to New York to persuade the RCA brass to let her produce her own albums without Porter as well as discontinue their duets, Dolly-watchers exchanged smug "I-told-you-so" looks. Even some of the local pickers, who number among Dolly's staunchest fans, became piqued when she announced she would no longer use studio musicians on her sessions, but would record only with her own group, Gypsy Fever. Since Dolly was virtually incommunicado with the press during this time (previously she had been one of the most cooperative and accessible

Dolly Parton goes pop but stays as sweet as she is: Above and near left, she triumphs at the 1976 CMA Awards Show with Male Vocalist of the Year Waylon Jennings (left) and, bearing her Female Vocalist of the Year trophy well, receives some advice from veteran pop "crossover" artist Charlie Rich. In the far left photo, she tapes one of her TV shows with L.A. country-pop stars (and Dolly fans) Linda Ronstadt and Emmylou Harris.

stars in Nashville), every move she made inspired speculation, second-guessing and more rumors. When *Esquire* sent a journalist to Nashville to do a cover story on country music's top three women (Tammy, Loretta and Dolly) they were told by Dolly's management that she would be unavailable for interviews unless the magazine wanted to devote its entire cover and story to Dolly. "We don't want her lumped in with those country singers," was the word that came back to *Esquire.*

"We all love Dolly, but right now we're puzzled 'cause we've been hearing things that just ain't like her. I hope she's not letting nobody change her or give her bad advice, 'cause she's always been one of the very nicest people in this business," Loretta Lynn commented.

Dolly finally decided to speak up in her own defense (with or without her new management's approval) but not before months of speculation had led to considerable misunderstanding. First she explained that it was a lack of time, not the desire to hide anything, that had kept her away from the press.

"If I had answered one rumor I would have had to answer them all," she sighed, "and there were so many, I wouldn't have had much time left for anything else. My schedule last Fall was ridiculous. The four months I had off, which I *was* ordered to take by my doctor because of throat problems, didn't help because when I went back to work it was more hectic than ever. I was doing concerts, taping my TV show in Nashville, producing my first album, trying to keep my writing up, and to be perfectly honest, it was just too much for me. I was putting in eighteen-hour days during the week, working the road weekends, and trying to re-organize my entire operation in between. There just wasn't any time left over for interviews or press conferences.

"The people who said I was going pop plain didn't understand. When they heard the word 'change' it flew through the country like a plague. Everything got so distorted and out of proportion I couldn't believe it. I meant I was changing things that were not right in my organization, not changing myself. What would I change into anyway?

A pumpkin at midnight? I'm so totally *me* it would scare you to death. I know myself very well and I don't fool myself. I know exactly what I can do, and that's just about anything I want to do, mainly because I'll work hard enough at it. I'll *believe* I can do it, then if I actually can't, I'll bluff my way through it. I can't change, but I *can* improve. And I can improve the things around me. What I'm after is my own musical unit. There are people out there who see this business as I do and I'm finding them, people who are unique in their own way and creative and want everything to be right like I do. I have always had big dreams and as I reach my goals the dreams get bigger. I had people around me who couldn't dream as big as me and it was turning my dreams into nightmares. I had to cut loose so I could dream free. What I am doing now is truly me, and if I offend people by being myself, then they don't love me very much anyway. All I'm trying to do is to be my *total* self, something I've never had the opportunity to do before. Now I am free to express myself totally. That doesn't mean I won't always do my 'back home' songs with banjos, fiddles and guitars, but I'll also continue to do other things. My songs are like children. They don't all look alike and they don't all sound alike. They don't all grow up to be the same thing, so I'm going to treat every one of them as an individual."

On stage, Dolly is a relaxed, warm, vivacious performer who has audiences (even non-country fans) eating out of her hand within minutes, but you have to spend time with her in person to fully appreciate her charisma, her intelligence and her beauty. Watching her on a stage, one is overwhelmed by the overall apparition—her hourglass figure revealed boldly in skin-hugging sequined costumes, her bales of blonde hair piled as high as she's wide—so that it's difficult to concentrate on her face. Take away all the make-up she keeps backstage in a metal tackle box, the wigs and hairpieces she won't be without, the gaudy costumes, and you have a woman of breathtaking beauty. She has a flawless complexion, large, wide-set, unwavering blue eyes, an aristocratically shaped nose, a sensuously curved mouth enhanced by deep dimples, and teeth so even and

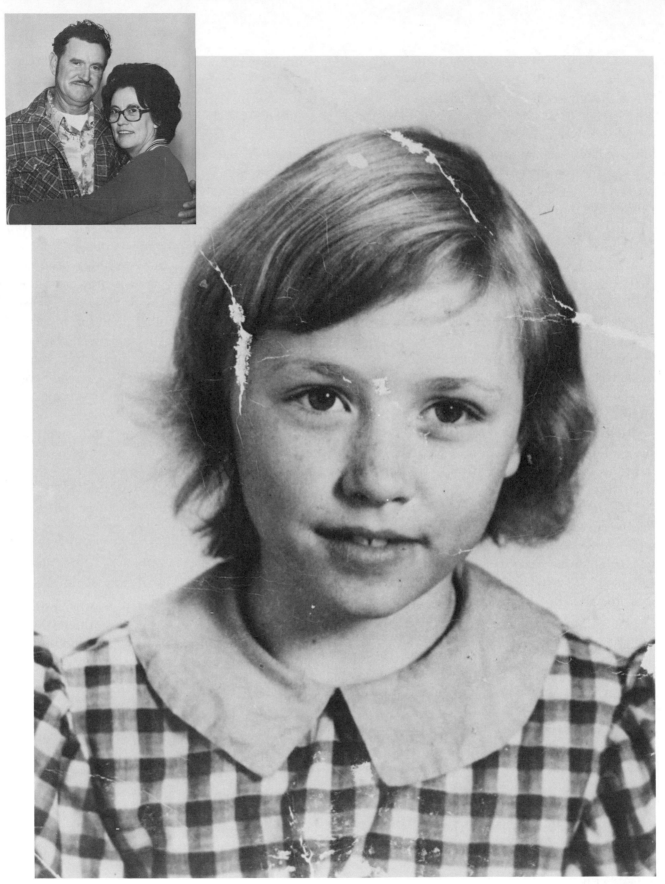

Dolly at about eight years old. "I was a homely little thing," she recalls, and says that "we slept four or five to a bed, and it didn't matter if you stopped wettin' 'cause somebody else was gonna pee on you anyway." Inset, Dolly's parents.

white she could make a living doing toothpaste commercials. Though her gaudy image belies the fact, she has the most beautiful face in country music, and if it weren't for her animation, her charm, her total lack of vanity, hers would be the kind of beauty that puts people off by its very perfection.

Dolly, however, tends to see herself as she did when still a child ("I was a homely little thing"). "I don't look this way out of ignorance," she says firmly. "I look this way because I like it. Anybody can look like a common Joe. I like looking like I came out of a fairy tale. I know I ain't in style, but I like to think I've got a style of my own. When I was real small, if someone came to our house who had a lipstick, I thought they was millionaires. If they had on a pretty sweater, or a shawl or something like that, I thought, 'Well, they've never had a trouble in their life.' I always thought I was ugly and I still do if I ain't got my paint and powder on. I won't go outta the house without it. My husband teases me and calls me Connie Complex. My hair and my clothes and all may be artificial, but it's another way of me being myself because I'm doing it because I *want* to, not for any other reason. Anyway, it's a part of an image now and I ain't gonna blow that. I *like* the image. If people don't accept me, I just figure they're as dumb as they think I am."

Dolly hasn't always been so impervious to criticism. Rumors and ridicule have become old acquaintances. She generated the former from her earliest years in country music, but she suffered the pain of the latter even as a child. One of her most famous songs, "Coat of Many Colors," tells the story of one experience when she went to school wearing a jacket made of scraps from the rag bag.

"My mother worked for weeks making that little coat because she wanted me to look nice to have my picture taken at school for the first time," Dolly recalls. "She had to sew each scrap together like patchwork before she could make it. I'd watch her working on it and she'd tell me how Joseph had a coat of many colors just like the one she was making me. I was so proud of it. But when I wore it to school the children teased me and

pulled at the jacket, calling it a 'rag top' and trying to unbutton it. I didn't have on no blouse underneath and I was so embarrassed I wanted to crawl in a hole and die. It hurt so much I couldn't talk about it for years. Finally as an adult I was able to write a song about it and get it out in the open. I've found that when I'm able to put the hurting things into my songs they don't hurt any more. It's better than a psychiatrist."

Dolly was the fourth of twelve children. She was born to Avie Lee and Robert Lee Parton on January 19th, 1946, in a two-room wooden shack deep in the Smokies near Sevierville, Tennessee. Her older sister, Willadeen Blalock, remembers it as a joyous occasion. "It snowed the night she was born, then the sky turned bright blue the next day. All the neighbors came from miles to see the new baby. She was the most beautiful baby I'd ever seen, the first in our family with blonde hair and fair, ivory skin."

Dolly's father eked a living out of the land, and her mother, who married at fifteen, was continuously tied to a new baby, barely getting one weaned before the next arrived. Like Loretta, Dolly knew a level of poverty most Americans can only imagine, but also like Loretta, she remembers her homelife as happy, cheerful, and filled with "singin' and pickin'." When Loretta and Dolly get together they don't swap woebegone stories of childhood deprivation. Instead they break one another up recalling incidents common to all who've grown up in rural poverty.

"Remember when company was coming how you'd shoo all the flies out real quick with a towel, then close the screen as fast as you could?" Dolly asks Loretta, who nods, laughing. "What about the outhouse? Did you have a one-holer or a two-holer?" Loretta asks. "One-holer," Dolly giggles. "Only rich folks had two-holers."

As a child Dolly had no opportunity for privacy ("We slept four and five to a bed and it didn't matter if you'd stopped wettin' 'cause somebody else was gonna pee on you anyway"), so she made her own private world inside her head. "I could be off in my own little fairyland anytime I wanted to, just by turning my mind to daydreaming," she says—but when she grew older

Scenes from Sevierville, Tennessee, where Dolly grew up in a two-room shack as the fourth of twelve children. The life was so far below the poverty level that when Dolly married, she took four of her younger brothers and sisters away from home and raised them herself in Nashville.

Dolly's high school years were plagued by the jibes of classmates who mocked her family's poverty and ridiculed her very firm conviction that one day she would move to Nashville and be a star. True to her word, Dolly left Sevierville the day she graduated from high school. Above, family photos from those teenage years.

and tried to share her dreams with friends and classmates, she faced more ridicule.

Willadeen remembers many occasions when children at school taunted Dolly. "She had her dreams of stardom from a very early age, and she wasn't shy about telling them. Where we lived back in the hills, *nobody* had dreams like that, so naturally the kids laughed. At her baccalaureate ceremony in high school the students were asked to get up and tell their plans for the future, and of course Dolly said she was going off to Nashville to become a singer. You could hear the sniggering all through the audience. I think the ridicule and teasing she took as a child might be one of the reasons she's so single-minded and determined today."

Dolly did leave for Nashville the day after graduation, just as she'd announced she would, with her meager belongings packed in a cardboard suitcase and a fistfull of songs scribbled in an old school notebook, and within hours of her arrival she had met the man who would become her "mystery husband."

Although they've been married now for more than a decade, so few people in the music business have met or even seen Dolly's husband, paving contractor Carl Dean, that there have actually been rumors that he doesn't exist at all, that Dolly "made him up" for the protection offered by the image of marriage without the restrictions of the real thing. The most popular story about her marriage, and the one repeated most often in the country music hang-outs around Nashville, is that it is

a "business arrangement only." Those who offer this explanation say that Dolly made a deal with Carl shortly before she went on the road with Porter Wagoner's show. "I hear she wanted a buffer against Porter's possessiveness," one musician speculated, echoing the frequently repeated theory, "so she offered Carl half her earnings in exchange for his name. They agreed to share the same house, but live separate lives."

Dolly's marriage inspires this kind of gossip because no other woman in country music (perhaps no other woman in the public eye) has a husband so elusive. According to her friends and acquaintances in the industry, her personal life with Carl goes beyond privacy. "It's invisible" is the way one observer puts it.

After three years of asking dozens of people in the business in Nashville—stars, producers, musicians, label executives, local press, publicists—I could find only four who remembered ever seeing Carl Dean: Tanya Tucker, who met him once at Dolly's house and describes him as "real nice;" singer Jeannie Pruett, who saw him once and says he is "as handsome as a movie star;" Fred Foster, President of Monument Records where Dolly first recorded, who remembers Carl as "very quiet and good-looking," and a former employee of Porter Wagoner's who recalls seeing Dean at one of the first TV tapings Dolly did with Porter about ten years ago. "He came in and stood off by himself and watched for a while," he recalls. "Then Dolly, who seemed surprised and nervous about his showing up at the studio, went over and talked to him,

Above, Dolly shines and stars in her own show after a long and painful disentanglement from Porter Wagoner. As her singing partner, producer, constant companion and overall career manager, Porter spent more time with Dolly than did her "invisible" husband. On the left, Porter and Dolly chat with CMA head Jo Walker and a newly arrived (and very hot) Johnny Rodriguez (1974).

but she didn't introduce him around. He only stayed about an hour, and none of us ever saw him there again."

Mysterious? Strange that in ten years of marriage, the husband of one of country music's biggest stars has never shown up at an awards banquet, even when his wife was nominated? Puzzling that they do absolutely no socializing with anyone in the business, have never invited her country music pals over for a meal or a drink? (Dolly says she's never given a dinner party in her life and wouldn't know how even if she wanted to.) Her peers find the relationship unusual enough to continue speculating about it, but Dolly doesn't consider her marriage strange at all, and when she sits there, eyeball to eyeball, explaining it patiently, she is so open, so charming, so persuasive, that she leaves the listener convinced her marriage is not so much a mystery as a miracle.

"When I came to Nashville the day after I graduated from high school, I had no thought in my mind but my music. I was eighteen years old and marriage was the last thing I wanted. I moved in with my aunt and uncle so I could watch their little boy while they both worked. I hadn't wanted to take time to wash my clothes before I left home, so that first day I walked down to the Wishy Washy laundromat to do my wash. After I got the clothes started I wandered around the block, looking over my new home town. Every little thing I saw was exciting because I'd never lived in a big city before. This fella drove by in a white '63 Chevy and when he saw me he honked and waved. Coming from the country, I was real friendly, so I waved back. He pulled over to the curb and we started talking. It was Carl and I thought he was the best-looking thing I'd ever seen in my life."

Dolly's mountain twang is softened by a cheerful little-girl voice which suggests enormous enthusiasm for life, even when she's being put on the spot. She is shrewd with the press. She becomes reserved rather than defensive if a question irritates her, but most of the time she sounds as though she's suppressing a giggle. Giggling is one of the things Dolly does best. Like Goldie Hawn, her's is so recognizable and contagious, it has become a kind of trademark.

"He asked me for a date, but I wouldn't get in the car with him or anything—we're not *that* friendly in the country—so I gave him my uncle's address and told him he could come callin' if he wanted to. He came by the next afternoon and every afternoon after that for a week. I wouldn't even invite him inside, 'cause my aunt and uncle weren't there, but we'd sit on the porch swing and talk while I watched after my cousin. Finally, when my aunt had a day off about a week later, we had our first date and he took me right to his house to meet his folks. By that time I already knew he was the man I wanted to marry 'cause something had just clicked when we met. But I wouldn't have pursued it 'cause I felt it wouldn't be fair for me to marry *anyone*, considering that my music was the first thing in my life.

"Then after we'd been dating a few months, Carl had to go into the Army. He was gone a couple of years, and it was really rough. I had gotten an apartment on my own and was trying to get my foot in the door of the business, living off canned beans and potted meat half the time and wondering when my break would come. I never doubted it would come, I just wanted it to hurry up. By the time Carl got home I had signed with Monument Records and they didn't think it was a good idea for me to get married, because if I got a chance to go on the road they were afraid a husband would stand in the way. But Carl and I had already worked all that out. I explained to him exactly how I felt about my music—that it wasn't something I did, it was *me*. I told him I had to do it, no matter what. And he knew that my music was what had brought me to Nashville in the first place and that I wasn't going to let anyone or anything stand in my way. I told him he had to be willing to accept this and that I had to know in my heart he could live with it, or we'd end up hurting one another and I couldn't stand that. He said, 'If that's what you want and that's what makes you happy, then that's what I want you to have.'

"I had to make sure that he understood that it was really going to happen, because I didn't want him thinking he was marrying a girl who would give up after a few years of trying to make

it. I said, 'It may be hard for you to visualize all of this now, but we won't have the kind of marriage other people have because my music is going to take me away from home a lot, and the bigger I get the more demands will be made on my time.' Any other man would probably have thought I was crazy—a kid from the hills talking about all these big plans as though they had already happened—but Carl accepted it. I told him I always dream big, but the difference is I *believe* it will come true because I put legs on my dreams the way people ought to put legs on their prayers.

"So we got married secretly in 1966, and it was a year before anybody knew about it. Then when the opportunity came to go on the road with Porter, they said, 'See, aren't you glad you're not married, or you couldn't go.' And I said, 'Well, I am married and I am going!'

"I think that first year of my marriage was the happiest of my life. I was more settled, more content, and my writing got a lot better. Not long after we married I won my first BMI Award for a song I'd written with my uncle, Bill Owens. We were invited to the big annual Awards Banquet, and I was very excited because I'd never been to one before, so Carl said he'd go with me. That was the first time he'd been to any industry function with me, and it was the last." Her suppressed giggle bubbles to the surface.

"I was really nervous, but Carl was worse off than I was. He didn't know anybody, or anything about the business, and he's a loner anyway, not a socializer at all. He really felt out of place that night. So after we got home he said, 'Now I know this is what you want for your life and I'm proud for you because I want you to have it if it makes you happy. But it don't make me happy and I don't want to be a part of it. I'm just too uncomfortable, and it's not *me*, and I can't get involved in it.' He said, 'If anything ever comes up in your business that I want to go to I'll tell you, but otherwise don't ask me to go because I don't want to be obligated and I don't want to feel I'm going to disappoint you when I say no.'

"Well, that was eleven years ago, and he hasn't asked to go to anything since and I haven't asked him, so it's worked out fine. Like all married people we get irritated with one another once in a while, mostly about things around the house or something. But I can honestly say that not once in all these years have we had one disagreement or argument or one case of hurt feelings over my music. Now, if other people see that as strange, it's only because they don't understand the way I think. I *expected* it to be this way. I *knew* it would be, because I know how to make things right by working at them, by *believing* it will be right. I thought you were supposed to be happy when you were married, so it doesn't surprise me at all that I am, or that my marriage has lasted. If it *hadn't* worked out, then I would have been surprised. I've been married only once and my husband has been married only once, and that's the way it will stay unless one of us dies. We're that sure of one another and what we have.

"I tease him sometimes and I say, 'If you ever have any thoughts about getting rid of me, you'd better think again 'cause I'm hanging on for dear life.' He knows there is no way he could ever lose me to someone else because I could never find another Carl. What I have in him . . . a person I can be so relaxed with, a person who understands and doesn't get jealous of the fact that my music takes up more time than he does. I'm not saying I could never be attracted to anyone else. Everybody sees an attraction sometimes in a person other than their husband or wife, but if I was ever tempted to do anything about it, all I'd have to do is think about how good I've got it at home and how I could never find that again."

"I don't mix my marriage and my music. I don't take problems from the business home with me. Half the time Carl doesn't even know what's going on in my career. I don't think he's ever even been on my bus. Right before I made so many changes in everything last year, we went on the first real vacation we've ever had alone together, and I told him a little bit about what I intended to do, but not to ask him or anything, just so he would know what was going on. But he's really not that interested. He doesn't even like the way I sing." She giggles again, apparently at ease with the fact that her husband is not a fan. "I know he loves me for the person I am, not the singer. Now

I'm so used to being away from home that if I spend more than a week in town, both Carl and I start to get restless. We're not together enough to pick each other apart. We're just together enough to be happy and keep it new.

"He still does his paving contracting work because he can't stand to be idle, and he takes care of the farm and he likes to buy old cars and fix them up into real antiques, so he has plenty to keep him busy. He's up every morning early and out doing something around the place in his old overalls, which is his favorite way to dress. He can fix anything, and if he can't fix it he can make a new one. He's a man who gets satisfaction from working with his hands."

Dolly and Carl have no children and don't intend to have any. "Our family was so big, we all had to help with the little ones," Dolly says, explaining her views on motherhood, "and after Carl and I married, four of my little brothers and sisters came to live with us and we raised them. So I feel like I've had the experience of being a mother. Carl has left the decision of having children up to me and I've chosen not to. Besides, I get the mothering experience from writing songs. It's like giving birth every time."

Dolly is generous with her family, but less so with herself. She has difficulty spending money on luxuries, and would rather buy gifts for her relatives than treat herself to something new. "When I go in to buy a new dress or sweater, I just have to buy one for someone else too," she confesses. "I feel too guilty if I don't. We grew up sharing everything, and it's still the way I think. My sister, Willadeen, used to work in the school cafeteria for twenty cents a day, or a hot lunch, whichever she wanted. All we had to carry for school lunches was cold biscuits, and we'd sit off by ourselves and eat 'cause we didn't want the other kids to make fun of what we'd brought. But my sister would take the twenty cents instead of a hot lunch, and then divide it between us so we could have a candy bar or something special like that. Mama didn't even know she did it. When you've grown up with so little and you get money, you either want to spend it all, or you feel guilty about spending it, and that's me. But as I'm able

to do more for my family—like buy Mama and Daddy a brick house—I'm gettin' better about it. Carl and I have so many people around our house, mostly my family, we call it 'the depot.' I never know who's gonna be there when I come home."

For seven years of her marriage to Carl Dean, Dolly spent more time in Porter Wagoner's company than she did with her husband. As an established star for more than twenty-five years, Porter had built-in audiences for both his live shows and his syndicated television show, which has been reaching approximately forty-five million viewers weekly since its debut in 1961. When Norma Jean, the vocalist who had been with him for years, decided to retire, Dolly welcomed the chance to replace her. They traveled on his bus to road dates for fifteen to twenty days a month, taped his television show and recorded together when they were in Nashville, attended industry functions together, wrote and published songs together; in fact, they did more together than most married couples. He guided her career in all areas, from advice to action, and he is credited with "creating" her sex-symbol image—the Marilyn Monroe of Country Music—a fantasy figure of blonde curls and giggles, bosom and bangles, earthiness and vulnerability. In their personal life they exchanged valuable gifts. He gave her diamond rings and Cadillacs, she gave him half her publishing firm. Many of their fans thought they were man and wife; most of their peers believed they were lovers.

Publicly both have always denied that their relationship was anything more than a business arrangement, but several people close to Porter in Nashville claim that he fell "head over heels in love" with Dolly. "All you had to do was see the way he looked at her to know how he felt," one man offered. "Porter has a big ego. Other girl singers he'd had on his show were more or less kept in the background. But he pushed Dolly right up front and instead of it being Porter Wagoner's show, with Dolly Parton, it became Porter and Dolly in everyone's minds, including his. I know he saw the relationship as going on and on and on because he used to talk of what they'd be doing when they got tired of the road. Porter never thought Dolly would leave him. He couldn't imagine it, 'cause he couldn't have left her.''

At one time Dolly was resentful if anyone hinted there might be more than a business relationship between her and Porter, but now that she has broken all ties with him, she has become more philosophical about the rumors.

"I guess it's only natural that people would think things about me and Porter considering we were so close. People have said Porter was having an affair with every girl he ever had on his show, so why should I be different?

"They thought he was my sugar daddy, and it really used to upset me, but I don't worry about it anymore. Time takes care of those things. People think what they want to no matter what you say, so there's no use worrying about it. But my husband always knew. That's the important thing. Carl always knew you couldn't be married to a man and be fooling around with another man all those years and not have your husband know.

"Porter did more for my career than anyone, and I'll be grateful to him as long as I live. Carl understands that as well as I do. He also understands that there was a strong love between me and Porter. It was a very unique relationship. Porter and me are a lot alike. Our music bound us very close together. We had as much respect for each other as we did love, even though we knew one another's bad points as well as good. But that don't mean we were lovers. I could fall asleep on the same bed with Porter and we'd never touch as male and female are supposed to do. You don't have to share sex to share love."

Dolly's first break from Porter came in the Spring of 1974 when she left both his road show and television show. At the time rumors were widespread in Nashville that he was so distraught when she told him she wouldn't be traveling with him any more that he went into a rage and threatened to kill her. Dolly confided to a friend that his possessiveness had become "terrifying." "I don't know how I'll get away from him without a big, messy blow-up," she reportedly said. The blow-up never came, however, and a few weeks later it was Porter, not Dolly, who made the public announcement that she was leaving him. He called a press conference to say it had always been his intention to send Dolly out on her own when

Above, Porter Wagoner in all his rhinestone glory. Though exposure on Porter's nationally syndicated TV show (left) was probably what "made" Dolly's career, she grew restless with the narrowness of the "Porter & Dolly" image.

she was ready, and now the time had come.

Only a few intimates know what actually went on behind the scenes during the period when Dolly was trying to make her break from Porter, but two of them gave the same account of what happened: Dolly told Porter she had to leave him, with or without his blessing, because her future and her ambition demanded it. When he balked, she pointed out that since he was going to lose her one way or the other, it would be to his advantage to make the announcement himself rather than letting it come from her. This way, she promised, they would have an amicable parting and he would still be producing her. So Porter made the announcement, followed by another some months later that he was quitting the road altogether to devote all his time to producing himself and Dolly, and to his television show.

The following year, when Dolly discovered her own organization, Dolly Parton Enterprises, was in management trouble, she went to Porter for advice. He offered her his own manager, Don Warden, calling another press conference to say: "Dolly and I have been so close personally and business-wise that she has always discussed all phases of her career with me and come to me for advice concerning her business matters, even since she has been on her own. Since Dolly has depended on me I felt the best thing I could ever do for her was to offer her a man that had worked twenty-two years for my career, Don Warden, because he's the most qualified and has the most knowledge . . . it will take three men to replace him in my organization." At the same conference he added that he would "continue to produce Dolly's records for RCA and negotiate her business with them."

But Porter, however, would actually produce only one more solo album for Dolly (he produced one other, a duet album, which has never been released) before she went to New York the following Summer without his knowledge to negotiate her own business with the label. She asked for and received permission to produce her own albums. During the same period she also dropped Warden, replacing him with the Hollywood management firm of Katz, Gallin and Cleary. Thus, the final

break from Porter had been achieved after more than twenty months of step-by-step disentanglement.

Though Dolly keeps insisting "We're still friends," Porter did not try to conceal his irritation and hurt when he told *Music City News* "Had I known that Dolly and RCA were going to come to the decision that they could go further without my production, I probably would not have quit the road. I won't take the blame for us having no more duet recordings. I was the father of them and I created the act. Dolly and RCA are reaching out for a broader market and I guess they thought our duets were too country for her. I think it was a huge mistake. I think the duets were a big part of her career, and I think that *I* was a big part of her career. I didn't even know about the new production arrangements until about two weeks after the decision had been reached."

The only business association remaining between Dolly and Porter is co-ownership of Fireside Recording Studios in Nashville, and a partnership in Owepar Publishing, which holds Dolly's valuable catalogue. Owepar was founded by Dolly and her uncle, Bill Owens, shortly after she came to Nashville. She gave Porter 50% of the company as a Christmas gift months before she told him she was going out on her own. It has been said that this was Dolly's way of buying off her conscience, and certainly it was a generous monetary compensation to the man who had done more than anyone to make her into a country music star. But Porter had already been a millionaire for years, so it is doubtful that more money compensated for less association with Dolly.

Severing her relationship with Porter had to be a traumatic experience for Dolly, but the way she did it, slowly and cautiously, offers interesting insight into her personality. Dolly has a steel-willed determination to get what she wants and the patience to ride things out until the time is right. Her close friends say she was miserable those last two years with Porter, itching to get on with her ever-widening career plans, and fearful that her timing would be off if she delayed too long. Respect and genuine love for Porter slowed her down, but didn't stop her.

Friends say that Dolly was "miserable" during the last two years of her partnership with Porter. Above, a reflective moment on the set of Porter's TV show. Right, Dolly free and triumphant.

Dolly -- "The Iron Butterfly" -- with Ronnie Milsap, another enthusiastic fan.

"With any long-term relationship that ends, there's got to be a certain amount of hurt and disappointment," she says truthfully. "And it's no different with Porter and me. But we are still good friends and he will always know how important he has been to me and my music. I know it might have seemed to some people that I made a fast turn-around in my career, but to me it all happened very slow because I've been working behind the scenes for so many years to make it happen. The way my working conditions were, I had to plan it carefully, and as it turned out it all paid off at once."

Porter is not the first mentor Dolly left when she felt it was time to move on. Her first break in Nashville came through Fred Foster, founder and President of Monument Records, who signed her to a contract after she'd been knocking on doors for nearly two years.

"Dolly was still under contract to me when Porter made her the offer to go on the road," Foster remembers. "She asked me what I thought of the idea. I told her the television exposure on his show would boost her career tremendously, and the girl he hired for the road also got to work the TV show. Even though Porter's girl singers had always played second fiddle to him on the shows, I felt Dolly had a magic quality that would come across on television and grab the public even if she didn't get much of the spotlight. I still think her greatest potential lies in television and movies, and that TV will eventually make her a superstar.

"Porter and I had a meeting after she decided to go with him about how we could best promote Dolly. I don't think he actually knew what he had at first, but when he realized her potential, he wanted to sign her to RCA so they could record together. The day she and her uncle, Bill Owens, came to see me to tell me she was leaving my label was one of the unhappiest days of my life. I've never had a bigger disappointment in this business than losing Dolly. She had been with me almost four years and I had come to think of her as the kid sister I never had. She was the most unique girl singer I'd ever seen—her sound, her wellspring of ideas, her single-minded dedication to her music, her great gift as a writer. I believed there was no limit to how far she could go. I had never run across a female artist with such immense potential. In fact, I'm surprised she hasn't broken out and crossed all the boundaries before now. I think Porter got her timetable all fouled up or she would already be a superstar outside of country music. I imagine it took her longer to get out of that situation than she anticipated. But she's on her way now and she'll still get to the top.

"Nothing stands in Dolly's way when she sets her mind to do something. She was very upset, very emotional, about leaving Monument, but she left nonetheless. I knew she was torn between loyalty to me and wanting to take an opportunity she felt she needed, so there was no way I could become angry with her. All I felt was a bitter disappointment, but of course time heals even that. Dolly has a way of leaving you with a good feeling even when you hate it that she's left. Instead of running roughshod over you she sort of steps around you, if you know what I mean. And that in itself is a talent."

This particular talent has earned Dolly the nickname "Iron Butterfly." She has been fascinated with butterflies since childhood, when anything colorful or shiny attracted her eye, even little stones turned over in fresh plowed earth. "I guess it was 'cause we didn't have nothing pretty," she says, "so I looked to nature for beauty. To me butterflies were fancy dressed-up girls going to a party." She wears sequined butterflies on her costumes, and has countless symbols sent to her by fans—from needlepoint butterflies to butterfly rings and necklaces.

"The butterfly doesn't hurt anything or anybody," she says. "It goes about its business and brings others pleasure while doing it 'cause just seeing one flying around makes people happy. I'd like to think of myself as bringing people happiness while I do my business, which is my music." But the butterfly's beauty also attracts the prey that devours it. Nature gave it no defenses to fend off its predators. In contrast, Dolly is a survivor, and if she is forced to do battle to get what she wants, then she will do it with a fierce determination to win—thus "Iron Butterfly."

Dolly is less vulnerable, more decisive, more completely in control of her life and her emotions than any woman in this book. Her friend Linda Ronstadt says that Dolly is the only person she's ever met who is "free of neurosis."

"Maybe it's because I have no negative side," Dolly suggests. "They teach 'Positive Thinking,' 'The Magic of Believing,' all that sort of thing today, but someone had to feel and know it worked in order to start the program. And I was like that, even as a child. I always knew what I had to do to get what I wanted. I knew when to walk in a room at the right time, what to say to a teacher, what I would be doing when I grew up. I happen to be one of those people born with all the faith you can imagine. A lot of it stems from my religious background and my grandfather, who was a preacher and a big influence on me, but it's also just a part of my true nature. I have a child's faith, an innocent faith. I remember the first time I was told that the Bible says *all* things are possible, not just some things. I felt a flush when I heard those words, as though they had been written just for me, and I couldn't have been more than five or six years old at the time. It was like a light went on in my brain. I *knew* it was true, that all things are possible if you go after them the right way. I thought, 'Well, then I can have whatever I want and I can do whatever I need to do,' and that is exactly the way I have lived my whole life. The thing that amazes me is that everybody doesn't realize the power you have if you believe this way.

"I know myself and I like myself and I'm content with what I am," she continues. "I have a solid foundation inside me because I had a good upbringing, a good mama and daddy. I know there are other people smarter than me, but I'm happy with what I am, so although I can be hurt sometimes, the things people say about me could never throw me off balance or make me doubt myself."

With all this confidence, Dolly cannot go to sleep at night unless there is a light on in the room —a throwback, she says, to childhood, when the same kids who taunted her about her "Coat of Many Colors" locked her in a dark school closet.

Some of the hurtful things people say to Dolly concern her close relationship with Judy Ogle, a friend since childhood. Judy is a slim, quiet girl who wears little or no make-up and dresses in unpretentious Levis and shirts. She is as plain as Dolly is flashy, and around strangers she appears to be as withdrawn as Dolly is outgoing. Her expression has that closed, guarded look not uncommon among hill people in remote Southern areas.

"I met Judy when we were seven years old," Dolly says. "Now, this is going to sound funny, but Carl, Judy—so many things in my life—have had that strange quality of having been pre-destined. The *minute* I laid eyes on her I *knew* she was going to be my friend for life. Mind you, we hadn't even *spoken*. There was an interlocking of our eyes, and I just *knew*. We were just two poor trashy-looking little kids, but I had my dreams and I shared them with her, and she believed in them just as strong as I did. We were together all through our growing-up years. She lived a couple of miles from me and we spent hours together wandering around the fields, playing in the creek, talking, sharing secrets. We had all our classes together in school. We made one of those childhood pacts to be friends forever, like when you cut your fingers and let the blood mingle. But even without doing that we knew we'd always be together.

"I came to Nashville the day after graduation as I'd always planned to do, and as soon as I had a place for Judy, she came too, and she's been here with me ever since. She lives at our house. She's like an extension of me, like my shadow. And I'm like an extension of her. We can look at one another and know what the other is thinking. She's devoted to my music and I'm devoted to her because of that. We never get tired of one another. Judy is the only person in the entire world I could spend 365 days a year with—seven days a week, twenty-four hours a day—and never even be aware of the fact, never be bored by it or feel I wanted to get away from her. We can be in the same room for hours and not say a word, because we're both preoccupied with something, but it's never un-

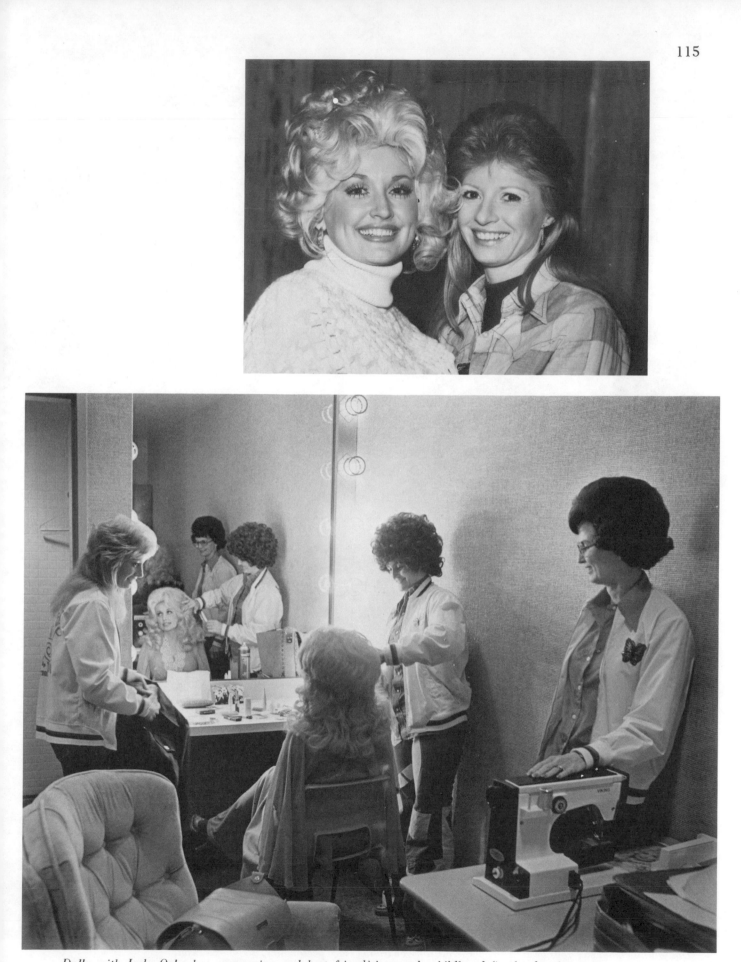

Dolly with Judy Ogle, her companion and best friend since early childhood (in the dressing room photo, Judy is on Dolly's left). Dolly's relationship with Judy, who lives in the Parton residence, is one subject for Music City's tireless gossip mill.

Dolly doing what she does best. This, her irresistibly charming stage personality, is the end result of a level of determination some find truly uncanny.

comfortable. I have other friends who are very dear to me and very close, but none so close as Judy. She knows as much about me as it's humanly possible to know about another person. She believes in my dreams as much as I do, and the Bible says that if two people agree upon the same thing with utter faith, it shall be done. Now why am I not supposed to have this friendship with Judy? What is wrong with it? Why do people insinuate there's something sick about it when it is really something beautiful? They say true friendship is a gift of God and that's the way Judy and I accept it. I feel sorry for people who look at it any other way."

Judy's presence goes beyond companionship, however. She handles countless chores and details —from secretarial to household—and saves Dolly time and aggravation, but she insists on remaining in the background. She is a natural target for interviewers who want real insight into Dolly because she knows her better than anyone else does, but she has never talked to the press and says she never will. One senses that Judy's unfailing support of Dolly's dreams and plans is at the core of their unusually strong bond. She is the only person who has shared each new dream along the way, constantly reinforcing Dolly's own belief that she can do anything she makes up her mind to do.

"Some of my dreams are so big they would scare you," Dolly says confidently. "And I see my goals more clearly all the time. In fact, when things start to get cluttered I write out my programs so I don't lose track of exactly where it is that I'm going, the things I intend to do, the things I *intend* to see happen. One of my goals is to write music for movies. What do they call it? Scoring? I want to score movies, and play in them too, but I want to write my own parts. I am a dreamer, but I am a do-er too, and all of my life there has been this strange thing within me that says 'do this' or 'do that.' Maybe it's common sense, or instinct, but I've always known exactly how far I could go in any situation, and I've always known when to move on. It's not like I make the plans so much as the plans are already made for me. I wait until I feel something is right and then I do it. I believe all this is leading to something far beyond country music or pop music or even entertainment. I think it will come to something I will use to help people help themselves because the bigger you get the more people you reach. I'm not a good Christian, but you don't have to be to let God work through you. I know one thing. Some day I am going to write a book on how to make faith work for you."

Dolly's faith is a powerful force which can actually be felt in her presence, but it's not so much religious faith as a faith in herself (though she often adds "with God's will" when revealing future goals). Most of her peers in Nashville share her belief in herself. Loretta Lynn says, "If Dolly tells you she's gonna make movies, look out, 'cause she'll make 'em," and Chet Atkins suggests that, "There's no limit to what she can do, where she can go. Her potential hasn't been tapped yet."

On the left, the final preparations for a Dolly appearance (the hair is a wig, and the woman in the foreground is Emmylou Harris). Above, one of Dolly's more everyday costumes.

Wherever Dolly's dreams take her, however, some things won't change. Her songwriting, admittedly the most important activity in her life, will always take top priority over other creative outlets. Unlike Loretta, who can go for long periods without writing at all, or Tammy, who writes when she needs to express a feeling or a thought, Dolly is like a computer programmed to produce continually. She writes as many as twenty songs in one day and has written literally thousands since she began at age five, even before she knew how to write letters. "My mother would write the words down for me," she remembers. "I made up songs about everything that happened in my life. It wasn't something I thought about doing. It was more like a compulsion."

The subject matter of Dolly's songs is more varied than that of the other female country writers, and her style ranges from storytelling tales as intricate as those of Marty Robbins or Tom T. Hall to sentimental love ballads as touching as Tammy's. She has written about abortion, religion, animals, children, love (both unrequited and fulfilled), fear, faith, birth, country life, jealousy, joy and motherhood. Her melodies don't always live up to her lyrics, but her poetry compensates in the vividly picturesque way she can set a mood or a scene within the confines of a few short lines. Many pop, rock and country music critics agree that she is probably the most talented female songwriter of the day. And as she matures, she is getting better, constantly stretching her talent and exploring new ways to communicate through her music.

When it was mentioned to one Nashville music critic that trying to define Dolly's complex personality is like going after a ghost with a butterfly net, he suggested the best insight could be found in her music. "If you study her songs, you're still left with a mystery in the end," he concluded, "but you realize just how complicated this woman is. In person Dolly's charm and naturalness mask the complexities. She appears as a vivacious, warm and witty person with this marvelous positive attitude toward herself and life in general. And she is all of that. But she is so much more, so much deeper and unfathomable that it boggles the mind to speculate about what actually does go on in the head beneath that mountain of blonde hair."

Now that all her old business ties are broken and Dolly is moving out in new directions, surrounded only by people who can "dream as big" as she can, many of her long-time country fans fear she will eventually leave their music behind as well. But Dolly vows this will never happen. "That's my roots," she says, "my very foundation. What I'm doing now is building on my foundation, and I want the freedom to build as high as my dreams will take me."

Nobody, including Dolly, knows how high this will be until she gets there. But her statement to Chet Flippo of *Rolling Stone* indicates that she is armed for anything: "I'm prepared for success and braced for failure. I don't expect failure at all, but I would be able to accept it because I would succeed in whatever I do eventually. There is a difference in being a failure and failing at things, and there is a difference in being a success and being successful, and I know the difference."

In Dolly's case the difference is attitude. Nobody with her adamative will to win could be considered a failure, even if they don't always appear to be winning. If a door closes in her face, Dolly will simply open another one. So far nothing has stood in her way for long—not family, not husband, not friends or business associates. Her drive blocks out all distractions like blinders on a horse; her ambition urges her on like the electric bunny pacing the greyhound. Dolly has less conflict in her life than Loretta, Tammy, June or Tanya because all her energies are harnessed into one area—her music, i.e. her career—but by their definition of the word, she also has less fun. Dolly would disagree. "My music brings me more pleasure than anything else in the world, so it's easy for me to devote myself to it. It is not necessarily bad that people don't understand what I'm doing now, but in a few years everybody will know. Talent isn't going to get me where I'm going. It's my faith and determination that will do it. I'm really not all that talented. I'm not a great singer —a lot of people can't stand the sound of my voice—and I don't know music technically. But what I create is totally from within, totally me. My biggest talent is being myself." ♥

"Lord, five years from now I want to own the moon."

TANYA

The pastoral setting of Tuckahoe Farms, bordered on one side by the Cumberland River and protected by lush green Tennessee hills on the other, provided an incongruous backdrop for a steady stream of cars and people cutting across the landscape towards a farmhouse outside which, on a long, heavily-laden buffet table, a huge ice-sculpted figure "18" melted slowly in the afternoon sun. It was Tanya Tucker's eighteenth birthday.

It was a festive event on a pretty day, and for any other teenager it would have been an eagerly awaited and joyously celebrated occasion—but Tanya, who joked that at least she wasn't "jail bait" any more, faced it with the nagging uncertainties most women don't feel until middle age begins looming on the horizon. Not even the fact that just days before *Record World*, *Billboard* and *Cashbox* had all voted her the Top Female Singles Artist of the Year did anything to quell the uneasy feeling that this day marked a turning point much more significant than a mere coming of age.

Her sixteenth birthday party had been the high point of her life. The date had coincided with her signing a multi-million dollar, five-year contract with MCA Records, and her father, Beau Tucker, had rented an entire carnival in Little Rock, inviting friends and press from all over the country. After presenting her with a "front money" check for more than a million dollars, Mike Maitland, the president of the label, had forever endeared himself to Tanya by getting into a rough and raucous bumper-car race with some of the younger guests.

During the ensuing two years she had watched her career begin to take on a life of its own, and the experience had been as fascinating as it had been rewarding, but she sensed that no matter what accomplishments lay ahead, the excitement of those "firsts" were behind her forever. That was not all, though. Two days before her eighteenth birthday Tanya tried, with difficulty, to put her feelings into words. "People are going to expect more of me now," she had blurted out finally, after toying in silence with a glass of soda for several minutes. "I'm not a little kid with a big voice anymore. I'm grown now. I'm just another singer. It's like I've lost my . . . my identification!

"Worrying about it may sound dumb, but in show business everybody has a gimmick, an image. It's the thing that identifies them. Dolly has that incredible body and all that hair; Tammy has her sad love songs and broken marriages; Loretta has all that stuff about being married so young and having babies before she knew where they came from, and June . . . well, June has all the whole Carter Family thing, plus she's got Johnny. Well, *my* image was this little girl with a gutsy voice singing about things little girls aren't supposed to know about. I mean, I was singing 'Don't Come Home A'Drinkin' at civic meetings when I was *nine* years old. It got a big reaction, coming from a kid, but I can't depend on that anymore."

Tanya's fears that day, though unfounded, were understandable. These were not the concerns of a novice in the business; these were the anxieties of a seasoned performer who had worked as hard as any adult to plan and build a career. The fact that she started before puberty had not made the climb any less arduous. Now she would have to face the test: Had audiences been coming all these years just to see a phenomenon, or was it her talent as an entertainer that brought them in?

It is clear to others that although at some point in Tanya's early career the crowds may have paid to see the paradox of a kid belting out songs about murder, sex, cheating and dying in a lusty, dark-brown voice, they stayed (and came back) to enjoy one of the most dynamic female performers in any music—country, rock or pop. But to Tanya, whose vision of herself as a performer is intrinsically linked to that "kid," the picture was out of focus. And only the coming months, perhaps years, would bring forth another sharp image.

"They'll be looking at me now for what I project as a singer," she reflected. "I've watched the biggest stars in the business, and I think I can do as good as they do if I try hard enough. I think I have the ability. Now I've just got to get out of there and give it all I've got."

In the past, what Tanya's got has been enough to leave lasting impressions. Even in the beginning, she didn't walk on a stage with a child's eagerness to beguile. Even then she marched out

The triumphal sixteenth birthday party of Tanya Tucker, country superstar. For the past two years, producer Billy Sherrill had been feeding her a string of ominously suggestive, powerful songs like "Blood Red and Going Down" and "Would You Lay With Me (In A Field Of Stone)." At this party, Tanya received a million-dollar-plus check from MCA, her new record label; it was her first move away from her phenomenally successful "jailbait" image.

Tanya at thirteen and already a sensation. When confronted with her husky, enormously power-ful voice and supreme confidence, audiences and music business veterans alike were thoroughly stunned.

with steel-willed determination to knock them off their seats—and more often than not, she did it.

"The first time I saw Tanya perform I was stunned," recalls John Kelly of Las Vegas, the entrepreneur and manager who handled her early in her career. "My wife, Judy Lynn, was head-lining the Arizona State Fair, and Sam Young of *Billboard* Magazine approached us as we were walking toward the stage door of the auditorium. He had this big grin on his face and he said, 'Boy, have I got something inside you're gonna like.' I asked what and he said, 'It's a little girl who just turned twelve and she wants to audition for you. And furthermore she wants you to put her on Judy's show!' Well, people in my business are constantly being asked to audition some kid, and we avoid it like the plague. It usually turns out embarrassing for everybody. So I said, 'That's real nice of you Sam. I guess you set this whole thing up, huh?' He was still grinning like he'd put one over, but he did tell me she was good, and that I ought to listen to her.

"Backstage, her brother Don came up and introduced himself, then introduced Tanya. I thought she was a cute little thing. Then she started singing and this big, sultry voice came out of a little girl's body. It was fascinating. She sang 'Muleskinner Blues' and 'There Goes My Everything' and she was cool as a cucumber and as confident as she could be. I'm telling you, that very first day, she had the guts of a Missouri mule and still does. In fact, guts is *one* thing that entire family is not short on! After she sang, Don asked me if I would put her on the show. I said I'd talk it over with Judy but I didn't think so because there were too many other things involved. An audience of eight thousand people had paid to see a professional show, and the fair manager might not like us putting an amateur on. Besides, I knew there were hundreds of parents out there who thought their kids could sing, and if Tanya went on, every one of them would be in touch with me the next day. But when I talked to Judy we decided to do it anyway.

"Tanya was excited when she found out she was going to perform, but she wasn't nervous.

Judy gave her a nice build-up on stage. Then Tanya walked out there in front of a packed auditorium just like she owned the place. She said to the band, 'Gimme a C,' stomped her foot three times, and took off. And she tore the house down!"

The *Arizona Republic*'s view of that show, dated November 9, 1970, read in part: "One bright spot on the program was an impromptu performance by Tanya Tucker, 12, of Willcox, who had auditioned for Miss Lynn just before the show. The Arizona girl has a very promising voice and nearly stole the show."

Tanya has been stealing shows consistently ever since. She commands a stage with such confidence, exuberance and gusto that reviewers have often called her "The female Elvis," a comparison she once relished but now finds annoying. One reviewer noted that "on a powerhouse rendition of 'Ain't That A Shame' Tucker ripped into the vocal with the kind of uninhibited enthusiasm the Beatles used to bring to Little Richard songs." If comparisons are going to be made, she's at least in heavy company.

Tanya is also, along with Johnny Rodriguez, credited with bringing masses of record-buying teen-agers, who fled to rock during the sixties, back to country music, but country music—as Loretta, Tammy, Dolly and June have known it— is not where Tanya wants to be.

"People don't call Elvis a country singer, even though that's where his roots are," she points out. "I don't like being compared to him because I want to be *me*, but I would like to be like him in one way. I want to sing it all. I want to be able to pack 'em in at any auditorium or arena in the world, because they've come to hear *my* music. And that should be any music my voice can handle. If your vocal chords won't let you reach out to other things, then I guess you have to stay in country, but I feel I can sing other music. I don't care *what* label it has.

"There was a time when I consciously imitated Elvis because he was my idol. I learned how to move on stage watching him. I'd never seen a girl imitate him, so I thought I'd try it. I wore tight leather-looking pants outfits, and put my head down like he does when I sang, so naturally all the press picked up on it. But I'm beginning to find my own style now and I don't want to be compared to anybody. I want to be myself, and I want everyone to like me. Luckily my record label and my producer are giving me the freedom to experiment."

Tanya's 1976 producer, Jerry Crutchfield, a Nashville independent, believes his artist *can* go anywhere she wants to go musically. But Billy Sherrill, her first producer and the one who guided her through a string of nine number one singles on Columbia, has grave doubts. "I think Tanya today is exactly what I thought she was when I first heard her six years ago—a very *good* country singer," he says. "She's also a very *lucky* country singer. Tanya's got talent and drive and a strong voice, but I've always believed that the songs are more important than any artist, and she's been very lucky in having the right songs picked for her. When I first signed her, everybody made a big thing about the fact that I had this little kid recording songs with almost necrophilic overtones, but it wasn't planned that way. Recently I picked up an almanac that had her listed in the country music section. It said something about her 'meteoric rise to fame, the 13-year-old who flooded the market with her gothic tales of horror,' and it's strange that she's remembered that way because it was never intended.

"It actually all came about because I couldn't get Bette Midler. I saw her sing 'Delta Dawn' on the *Tonight Show* and the song knocked me out. That first line, 'She's forty-one and her Daddy still calls her baby,' *grabbed* me. But I knew Midler had just signed to another label, so I thought, 'At least I can have the song,' and I spent half the night calling New York to find out who had written it. Turned out to be Alex Harvey, an old buddy of mine right here in Nashville. I had signed Tanya a few weeks before but hadn't recorded her yet because I hadn't found the right material. I knew the kiss of death would be to take this kid and record her singing 'Here Comes Santa Claus,' so I was looking for something different and 'Delta Dawn' was it. The song was perfect for Tanya—deep vibratto, gutsy sound, heavy words—and it turned out to be one of those beautiful cosmic moments when the right song and the right artist were brought together. When the record started to climb the charts, they wanted to promote Tanya as a kid, but I disagreed. I said, 'As far as the radio stations are concerned, she's a seven-inch record. They all look alike to a jock. Let's sell her voice, not her age.' But the age thing made for an angle, so they used it. Then songwriters started sending me material for her along the same lines. I never wrote for Tanya like I did for Tammy, so I had to rely on the good writers to send me stuff. And they sent rough stories— bloodshed and broken hearts—but *good* songs. You don't pitch 'Stand By Your Man' to somebody just comin' off 'Blood Red And Going Down.' I had no intention of staying in that vein, but she left the label before we had a chance to try other things. It's hard to argue with a nine Number-One winning streak."

There was talk along Music Row that one of the reasons Beau Tucker took his daughter away from Billy and Columbia and signed her with MCA was that he didn't approve of the type of material she'd been recording, especially her last hit single on that label, 'Will You Lay With Me (In A Field of Stone).'

Beau denies this. "I could never give Billy Sherrill enough credit for what he did for Tanya's career," he says. "We didn't leave Billy, we left the label. MCA made us a better offer. It was as simple as that. And by the time Columbia got around to matching it, it was too late." He does insinuate, however, that they wondered whether Tanya's music was getting in a rut (albeit a very successful rut) with Billy, and questioned whether "new directions" would have been possible with him as producer.

If by "new direction" Beau means a cross-over into the pop field, he was probably right to question Billy's intentions. Certainly they wouldn't have found in Sherrill the enthusiasm expressed by Jerry Cruthfield when he talks of Tanya's future as a pop star. "Tanya has *unlimited* potential as an all-around entertainer," says Crutchfield. "She has strong country roots and that's good, but in my opinion she has fewer limits than any

The "Female Elvis" in action. By the time she was fifteen-going-on-sixteen, Tanya was performing a purebred sweat-and-sex appeal rock & roll show. On the right, she gets advice from her father. When pushed, Beau admits to having been uncomfortable with his daughter's image.

woman singing in our business right now. Timing is the most important consideration in a career. Tanya has been very successful with the material Sherrill picked for her, but she had peaked. That kind of material could not have given her the momentum to boost her into broader areas. We're not going to pick material that will be a drastic departure because we don't want to do anything to alienate the country fans. We want songs that will not only be acceptable and desirable to them, but will also say to the other side, 'Tanya Tucker has something for everybody.'

"When I began producing Tanya I didn't know so much what type of songs I *would* record as what I *wouldn't*. I was *not* going to pick any of those hot, sweaty, earthy Tobacco Road tunes that had given her a certain image when she was with Columbia. At this point I've cut three consecutive number one singles with Tanya—'I Don't Believe My Heart Can Take Another You,' 'You Got Me To Hold On To,' and 'Here's Some Love' —and she has such momentum now that I'm more concerned about pacing than anything else. We know where we're going. We just don't want to get there too fast."

Beau Tucker, a big, curly-haired man with a calm manner, expresses the same sentiments. "I'm not worried about how big Tanya's gonna get. She'll get as big as she wants to. I'm only worried about how fast it's coming. I wish things could slow down a little bit."

The only person who doesn't think her career is moving too fast is Tanya herself. "Everybody says I started in the business so young, 'cause I was only twelve," she says. "Well, to me, that was late. I knew what I wanted to do from the time I was eight, and by the time I was nine I had started making plans and working toward my goals. Sometimes it worries me that I can see so far ahead of everybody else. I've always been the type who wanted something before I could get it. That's why the first two or three years in this business were so hard for me. Ages thirteen, fourteen and fifteen were the roughest years because I was breaking into the business, learning what I needed to know about things behind the scenes, having to do bad shows because I couldn't afford a decent

band, taking bookings where you couldn't depend on the sound system—all those things really got to me. I wanted to jump right up there and work the top places without taking the steps along the way. I still fight with Daddy about bookings. I'll say, 'Why did you book me here again? I played here last year and the sound was bad and they didn't promote it right,' or something, and he'll sit me down and explain how you have to crawl before you can walk. I listen to him, but I don't always like what I hear."

The relationship between Tanya and her father has been the subject of speculation and gossip ever since the two hit Music Row in 1970, when songwriter Dee (Delores) Fuller took them to Billy Sherrill. When a parent is as consistently pushy about a child's career as Beau has been about Tanya's, the easy assumption is that the young person is being shoved into show business for the ego and/or financial gratification of Mama or Daddy. Beau has been accused of using Tanya's talents to line his pockets with gold, of pushing her into a world too competitive for children, of cheating her of a normal adolescence and of not giving a fig about her education. But most of Beau's critics are people in the business who have had to deal with him to get to Tanya, and few of them like him. Upon close examination, the accusations don't hold up. You only need to spend ten minutes with Tanya Tucker to know that nobody pushed her anywhere. She's been in the lead all the way, and if anything, the rest of the family has had to hustle to keep up. Tanya started working on her father, trying to persuade him to help her become a singer, two years before *he* actually made a move. And given her talent and temperament (impatient, tenaciously ambitious) it is very doubtful whether she could have had a "normal" adolescence under any circumstances. As she points out, "Entertainers are not *normal* people to begin with."

Beau did try to persuade her to continue her education (she dropped out of school in the ninth grade), but Tanya won him over by convincing him she couldn't learn about her business any place except out there doing it. "One of my classes was called 'Careers,' " she remembers. "Every-

At her sixteenth birthday party, Tanya poses with
Mike Maitland, the MCA Records vice-president who
handed her the million-plus check, and her father
Beau Tucker, who works full time on her career.
Beau has been accused of pushing Tanya too hard in
the cause of the family bankbook, but a closer look
at Tanya seems to suggest that it may be she who is
pushing him.   On the right, mutual affection with
Mike Maitland.

The evolution of the superstar: On the facing page, Tanya at twelve, when she first began turning record company executives to jelly; above, at an early fourteen, after producer Billy Sherrill had put her together with "Delta Dawn," her first big hit; on the right, at sixteen, when the bloody songs began to give way to more conventional country material; in the top photo, at eighteen, with a pop career off and rolling and quite a few doubts about the future.

body sat around trying to decide what they wanted to be when they grew up and how to go about doing it. I couldn't relate to that at all. I not only knew what I wanted to be, I was already working at it on weekends and vacations, and I had had two hit records."

Tanya's money is another consideration. Nobody but Beau himself will ever know how much of his drive to help his daughter succeed has been motivated by a craving for the financial security he never knew as a child, but even if it's been the prime factor (and Beau says it has not), it would not be a despicable motivation. "If I was just interested in the money I sure missed out on a lot of it by turning down things—like movie offers—I didn't think were good for Tanya's overall career," he says. "One producer offered a lot of money for her to do a nude scene. I just looked at him like he was crazy, then I told him off."

If Beau resents this line of questioning he doesn't show it. He doesn't get defensive, and he doesn't try to change the subject: "One of the good things about me being Tanya's manager is that the money is *not* what I'm most concerned about. This is not your regular manager-singer relationship we're talking about. This is my *daughter*. And if you'd ask me which I'd rather be known as—the greatest manager in the world, or the greatest Daddy—I'd take Daddy in a second. I'm *glad* Tanya makes money, glad my family doesn't have to live the way I did as a kid, glad I know they'll never go hungry. But they never went hungry before she started singing, either. We weren't rich and we didn't have any luxuries, but there was always food on the table and a roof over our heads. Myself, I'm not a big money spender. Never have been, but I do like to see my family comfortable. It makes me feel good to see them have the things I never had. I grew up in 'Nowhere,' Oklahoma, the seventh child in a family of nine. My Daddy ran off when I was six and things went from bad to worse. I was only fifteen when I got married but I swore then my family would never do without the way we did as kids. I had to leave school after the fifth grade and go to work full time, and I've done about everything you can name. But I

was always a good promoter—a natural-born promoter—so when my little girl showed me she had the potential, the talent to become a star, and the determination to stick to it until she got there, promoting her seemed like the obvious thing to do. And of course it worked out better than any of us expected. Tanya was a millionaire before she was sixteen."

"I do worry about her money, but not in the way some folks think. I want to make sure she has a financially secure future no matter what happens in the business. Most of her money is in a trust fund. Twenty years from now Tanya will be a very rich woman if that money is protected along the way, and that's what I worry about. She has enough money so that she ought to be allowed a mistake or two without losing everything. If she marries the wrong man, then I want her to have something to fall back on. The day is gonna come when she'll have to step down and let the next singer come up, and when that happens I want her to feel she's been as far as she wanted to go. I want her to have the money to live any way she wants to the rest of her life."

It would not be possible to gain real insight into Tanya without understanding her father, for without his example of tenacity, optimism, and bull-headed faith, there would be no Tanya as she is today.

Jesse Tucker (the "Beau" evolved from "Sonny Boy," a nickname given him by a neighbor when he was a child) was born during the Depression to a family whose future appeared as grim as the times they lived in. The fact that he emerged a man of confidence and optimism is a minor miracle. After his father abandoned the family, he and his mother and eight brothers and sisters lived a hand-to-mouth existence, and as often as not the hand that reached the mouth was empty. To this day Beau hasn't forgotten what it was like to go to bed hungry. He went to work full-time at twelve, and by the time he was fourteen he was doing a man's job in a production plant.

He first met Tanya's mother, Juanita, in Denver, Texas, where his family had migrated to pick cotton. They were both in grammar school and Juanita didn't like him ("He stole cookies out of my lunch pail and he was too brash," she recalls), but after he quit school and went away to work, he changed. "When he came back, he was different," she says. "He was a man."

A man at fourteen, a husband at fifteen, a father at sixteen—Beau knew all about getting an early start.

Tanya's birth, on October 18, 1958, was a joyous occasion, even though the last thing the Tuckers needed was another mouth to feed. The country was going through an economic recession that had hit the dry, dusty West Texas town of Denver with a lot more impact than was being felt in Eisenhower's Washington. There, cocktail party chatter focused on the successful launching of the first U.S. satellite, and Vladimir Nabokov's shocking runaway bestseller, *Lolita*, but back in Denver, a place so barren and flat that the oil wells were a landscape relief, the family—Beau, Juanita, Don (14), La Costa (8), and the newborn Tanya—lived in a small trailer, quarters so close that they *had* to get along well together. There were no luxuries, but they were healthy and well-fed, which was better than Beau's childhood had been. Even though they had already lived in scores of West Texas towns, pulling up stakes whenever a new wildcatting oil job opened up, Beau had not lost faith in his future. Nomadic by nature, adventurous by spirit and a man of such vast dreams and schemes he sometimes frightened his complacent wife, Tucker reasoned that if he didn't find his fortune one place, the next opportunity must be just over the horizon and down the highway. By the time Tanya was eight months old they had hitched up the trailer to a battered old jalopy and moved to Willcox, Arizona, where Beau was confident things would be better.

La Costa remembers her father in those years as "a hard worker who could always get a job. I remember once he had to go to another town to get work, and after only a week the boss was so impressed with him, he let Daddy borrow his car to come home and visit us."

Beau enjoyed his children more than most fathers and took enormous pride in their smallest accomplishments. Donald was friendly and easy-going, La Costa sweet and obedient, and the baby, Tanya, an affectionate, gregarious, strong-willed little show-off who had the entire family eating out of her hand by the time she was three.

"She was a Daddy's girl right from the start," recalls La Costa, who is now a singing star in her own right with Capitol Records. "She was feisty and had a lot of spunk even when she was really small. And she could always do funny things to make us laugh."

By the time Tanya was six or seven, she noticed that La Costa (or, as her family calls her, simply "Costa"), was getting a lot of Daddy's attention around her house by singing to him. She remembers going to her father and saying, "I can sing too, Daddy," and having him laughingly tell her she couldn't sing her way out of a paper sack. "I decided to show him," she says. "I backed off and gave it all I had, and when I finished he looked at me kinda funny and said, 'Boy, that sounded pretty good. Sing me another one!'"

That may have been the precise moment when the seed for Tanya's future was silently planted in both their minds. Regardless, by the time she reached the sixth grade, Beau was convinced he had sired a future star. "I believed it because she convinced me," he says now. "It was more than her voice. It was her attitude, her determination, that gave me faith. She was never like other kids, never interested in the same things. From the time she got the idea in her head that she was going to become a singer, that's all she thought about."

Beau realized they would have to get out of Willcox, a one-radio-station town with no place to showcase new talent, if they were going to put Tanya's determination and his faith to work. "We're not going to live forever," he told his family. "If we're going to do this thing, let's get on with it." And as easily as that he quit his job and moved them to Phoenix.

The most unusual aspect of Tanya's success story is Beau's repeated willingness (it was to happen many times over the next few years) to forsake the security of a job on the highly improbable chance that he could guide an adolescent to stardom in a business to which he had never been exposed and about which he knew absolutely nothing. Spelled out that way it sounds so illogical, so irrational, so *impractical* that one can't help but wonder whether Beau Tucker was a madman or a fool. He proved, of course, that he was neither. And at the time, the plan seemed perfectly logical to him: Tanya had talent. Tanya wanted to be a singing star. Beau had Tanya. Beau wanted a better life for himself and his family. Why not give Tanya what she wanted and get what he wanted at the same time? The odds against their succeeding may have appeared ridiculously high to others (Costa recalls that some of the Willcox neighbors "thought Daddy was crazy"), but to a gambler of Beau's class, that only made the challenge more exciting.

"I've always been a go-for-broke guy," he explains. "My wife got scared sometimes, but I never did. Back when I was a kid I'd walk into a dice game with a week's pay and lay it all on the line. I wouldn't have thought of betting a dollar. If I lost, I lost. But when I won, I really won something." Tanya remembers a time in Phoenix when her father took a few hundred dollars he'd earned on a construction job to Vegas and bet it all on Keno. "He won something like $1100," she tells proudly, "and brought it all home and spent it on cutting demo tapes on me so he'd have something to take around to people in the business."

In Phoenix, things were not moving along fast enough to suit Tanya. Beau was out hustling the tapes when he could—sometimes even as far away as Vegas and Nashville—but the dialogue usually went something like this:

Tucker: "I've got this tape I want you to hear of this little girl who sings better'n Brenda Lee."

Cornered Target: "Yeah, who is she?"

Tucker: "My daughter."

Cornered Target: "Oh, that's real nice. My kid sings too . . . guess they all do nowadays. Why don't you just leave the tape?"

"If I had one person tell me their kid sang too, I must have had a hundred," Beau recalls. "Nobody wanted to listen, even though Tanya had appeared on quite a few local shows by then. I had helped her and Costa get a group together, and they did school shows and civic things."

In August of 1970 the Tuckers were broke and Beau was forced to accept a construction job in St. George, Utah. He couldn't turn down the nine dollars an hour, even though he felt their chances of launching Tanya's career from that remote area were practically non-existent. Ironically, however, the fact that they were living in Utah did help them get the first big break. Only a few months after they settled in, Tanya had persuaded her father to make the three hundred-mile drive back to Phoenix so she could try to get on the Judy Lynn State Fair Show. John Kelly remembers that the thing that persuaded him to let Tanya perform was the fact that the family had driven all night to get there from Utah, and "I felt kinda sorry for them."

Tanya's appearance on that show not only marked the first big turning point in her career, but was also the beginning of a turbulent three-year association between Kelly and Tucker. "When I got back to my office in Las Vegas after the fair, there was a letter waiting for me from Tanya," Kelly says. "She thanked me and asked me if I could get her on any more shows. Then Beau, whom I had not met personally at that point, started calling and asking if I'd handle Tanya. I turned him down because I had my hands full with Judy and other clients, and I know what a job it is to launch a career. The next thing I knew he'd moved the family to Vegas, and was in my office nearly every day. He finally wore me down and I agreed to handle her, but he was the hardest man to deal with I've ever run across. Nothing satisfied him. He drove one of my secretaries right into a nervous breakdown, and I'm not exaggerating. Her doctor will verify that. All of us in the office had to have our home numbers changed because he would call you any time of the night and keep you on the phone for hours, just nit-picking about things.

"They met Dee Fuller, a songwriter, and she introduced them to Billy Sherrill when he came to town on business. She got Billy to listen to a tape of Tanya's and he agreed to sign her. After 'Delta Dawn' came out we put the entire office on promoting that record. We wrote every disc jockey in the country and when it hit big, I thought Beau would lay off and be easier to deal with, but

Tanya with LaCosta, the big sister for whom Beau planned stardom before Tanya's grab for the spotlight. Today, LaCosta is also a successful recording artist.

TANYA TUCKER

JOHN KELLY & ASSOCIATES
P. O. Box 14927
Las Vegas, Nevada 89114
Phone: AC 702 451-1041

One of ex-manager John Kelly's publicity photographs for Tanya, then thirteen. Kelly recalls that he was glad to get rid of the Tuckers as clients, claiming that Beau caused his secretary a nervous breakdown by "constant nit-picking" but bemoaning the loss of Tanya herself, "a brilliant girl."

he got worse.

"They were with me until August of 1974, and when they finally bought out my contract I was glad to get rid of them—well, not Tanya. Tanya is a brilliant girl. I think if Beau would let her alone she could be the biggest thing in the country right now. I don't buy all this business about the things he gave up for Tanya's career. As far as I could see, he never had nothing to give up. But he's her Daddy and she'll stick up for him every time, even though I've seen them fight like cats and dogs. I remember one night in New York not long before they left me when Beau and her had an argument and he told me she was just gettin' to be too much to handle. She was doing more and more as she pleased as she got older. She'll take over her own management one of these days and I think Beau's afraid of that. He oughta be. She knows more'n he does about the business now.

"I've been around a lot of young talent, but I've never seen any kid with the confidence Tanya had. One time in New York she was doing a Johnny Cash TV show . . . she was about thirteen . . . and they had a twenty-seven-piece orchestra with a famous conductor in charge. They started playing her intro for a take and she stalked out on stage and called, 'No, No, *No*, that's not what I want. I want *this*' and she stomped her foot to the rhythm and went 'da *boom*, da *boom*, da *boom*.' Remember, this is a girl with no musical training at all. The conductor almost dropped his baton, but she got what she wanted."

Tanya has never been shy about asking for what she wanted, nor has she ever been hesitant about working to get it. Her latest acquisition, "Tuckahoe," her half-million-dollar, 220-acre farm outside Nashville, is the family's first real home, her "dream place." Tanya grew up living in trailers and cramped apartments, and vowed she'd someday own a farm with land "further than the eye could see." The property boasts four houses (her brother Don, his wife, and small son live in one, and she hopes Costa and her husband, Darrell Sorensen, will someday occupy one of the others). There's also a huge brick barn with a silver roof and curtained cottage windows. Even her horses live better than her family once did.

Fruit trees border the rich pastureland where the expensive pure-bred animals graze contentedly or frolic and play.

There's understandable pride in her voice as Tanya shows a visitor around the place. She lures a favorite horse to the pasture gate by sweet-talking him, then leads him to the barn where she saddles him up with the ease of a stable boy and the affection of a doting mama. She sits straight in the saddle, riding with the grace and confidence of an expert equestrian, her body and the animal's in perfect rhythm as they canter off across the pasture toward the river. These are the times, the only times, Tanya says, when she is able to push her career out of her mind and find total relaxation.

While Tanya gallops across the countryside, her mother, a soft-spoken, gentle woman with a sweet smile and open manner, is back at the main house going over brochures of furniture she wants to order for the family room. Beau is having a business meeting in another part of the one-story brick house and Tanya's brother, Don, has dropped in with his three-year-old son, Lacon, the apple of "Aunt Tanya's" eye.

When Tanya returns from her ride, aglow and invigorated, Lacon runs into her arms giggling and squealing in delight. She talks to Don about a horse she noticed limping, chats with her mother about the furniture and fondles one of her four dogs, a precocious new puppy named Alpha Beth. The atmosphere is congenial and relaxed, but a visitor senses that Tanya's good mood sets the tone for the others.

Leading the way to the privacy of the dining room, she sits in typical teen-age slouch as she talks about her life, displaying youthful ebullience one minute and adult caution the next.

"My horses are my pride and joy," she says enthusiastically. "I have five on the farm, two in Oklahoma being trained for the cutting horse Futurity in Ft. Worth, and another two in Alabama training for Western Pleasure show. The ones in Oklahoma are my best. They're both worth close to $30,000 apiece, a stud and a filly. Breeding horses is kinda like building an artist's career. You hope for a lot of wins, then you find a hot

Tanya at ease, forgetting the music business. These shots were taken in Nevada before the Tuckers moved to Nashville and bought "Tuckahoe," their dream farm where Tanya now keeps a fortune in thoroughbred horses.

stud to give you the best colts so you can get top prices. It's like hoping for a hit record so you can get top prices at bookings.''

She stops suddenly, chiding herself for relating horses to her career. "I've got to watch that," she explains. "We had a family talk about it last night at dinner—this habit we're getting into of talking business so much at home. It can get a hold on you if you let it and pretty soon you start getting above reality, like Mick Jagger and Elvis have. There's no reality for them anymore. I mean, sure we all love the lights and the applause and the excitement, but you have to have basics too, you have to stay in touch with reality. This farm is my reality. It's the place where I can get away from the business. It's also the place where I can get off alone and think. I spend most of my time traveling with nine people—my Daddy, five musicians and three back-up singers. I'm never alone . . . even if I go shopping somebody goes along 'cause Daddy has always worried about kidnappers. So going off riding alone where you don't see another soul is very soothing to me. You have to have something like that or this business can really mess your head up.''

Throughout her most impressionable years, Tanya has had the opportunity to observe "messed up" performers at close range, and she's determined to avoid the traps others have fallen into.

"Most artists treat themselves bad," she says. "They'll stay up all night partying, drinking, taking drugs. They'll book a string of one-nighters so far apart they're traveling till show time with not enough chance to rest, so they say, 'Oh well, if I take this little pill I'll feel like going on tonight.' If a performer treats himself right in the first place, those problems don't come up.

"I've never even tried marijuana. But I don't think that's any worse than the parent who sits there drinking whiskey telling his kid to stay away from grass. Liquor will kill you quicker'n anything. The reason I haven't tried dope is because I don't feel the need to reach outside myself to get high. Man, just walking on a stage when everything's going right makes me feel as high as I ever want to be. And my pride wouldn't let me take pills to get up for a performance. I want to feel

I've done it on my *natural* ability.

"I guess another reason I haven't smoked grass is because everybody else does it. I have this driving urge to be different," she smiles. "It's been with me all my life. I was the outsider at school, but I liked it. I *wanted* to be different. I've always been on another level from kids my own age. I knew things earlier—things about life and how to get what you want.''

Much has been written about Tanya's "lost childhood" and it's a subject that rankles her. "I had the best imaginable childhood," she says. "I've been surrounded by love and attention for as long as I can remember. That's one of the reasons I'm so reluctant to grow up. I can't imagine that being an adult is half as nice. No outsider can understand how close our family really is. We have our fights, just like anybody, but the *family* is the most important thing to every one of us. I mean, if I threw it all away tomorrow, I could start again and get it all back because I've got the family, the foundation.

"I know girls my age who hate their parents and want to move away from home as soon as they can. I feel sorry for them. My parents," she laughs suddenly, "would literally have to *kick* me out of here. And I'm with my folks a lot more than most kids. Mom used to go on the road a lot, but I like it better when she stays here and keeps it nice for me to come home to. An artist needs that.''

As if on cue, Tanya's mother walks into the dining room to offer refreshments, planting a kiss on her daughter's head before she leaves.

"I feel kinda sorry for the guy I marry," Tanya muses aloud after the door is closed. "He'll have a heck of a time breaking through the barriers of this family. Both my sister and my brother are married, and it hasn't been done yet. Costa's husband manages her now. Dad and I started her out when she decided she wanted to get into the business. He took her to Capitol and got her a contract, and worked with her for a year, but then her husband decided he wanted to take over. I think it hurt Dad's feelings, but I'm a full-time job anyway, and Costa's doing great. We're really proud of her.''

Tanya, whose style and ideology fall somewhere all her own between the warring factions of country music, makes a point to Willie Nelson, chief Outlaw.

One might think this was the older sister talking about the younger instead of vice versa, but Costa admits that Tanya was ready for the business long before she was.

"I remember when she was about nine and Mel Tillis came to the Cochise County Fair," she says. "She went right up to him and asked him if she could sing him a song. He was so charmed by the boldness of this little kid that he put her on his show. I could have never done anything like that. I didn't think show business sounded like a very stable career anyway. I went on to college and finished my education and got married and it wasn't until about two years ago that I felt ready in my own head to try it. Naturally I went to Daddy first. He got things started, then Darrell and I thought it was time for us to be on our own. It's hard for Daddy to realize I'm a wife now too. Anyway, I'd rather have him for a Daddy than a manager. I can enjoy him more that way."

Costa strongly denies that there has been any sibling rivalry regarding two careers in the family, and Tanya concurs. "Costa was my idol when I was growing up, my shining example," she says. "I wanted Daddy to help her all he could. It didn't cause any friction within the *family* when her husband took over." She seems to be implying that Costa's husband is still an outsider in the family. "Besides, Daddy's got his hands full with me," she adds.

Both Beau and Juanita say Tanya has been a "handful" since the day she was born. "She was my easiest delivery," Juanita recalls, "but by far the hardest to raise. She was so *active.* You couldn't turn your back on her a minute or she'd be into something else."

This is still a characteristic trait of Tanya's personality. No accomplishment satisfies her for long. "Now that I've got a good band and my act is coming together the way I want it, and I'm branching out in my music, I want to start writing and eventually I'll produce," she says. "But not until I know enough to be *great* at it. I want to make movies too, Disney-type movies that the whole family can see. I feel like I'm just getting started because up until now I've been learning and working to get to the point where you have enough know-how and power to get the things you want. Now when I do a session I say 'I want so-and-so on steel and a drummer on this song, and a vocal group on that one.' And they listen.

"I've been in this business six years now and I'm getting to where I know what *I* want, and they can't overlook that anymore the way they used to. But you have to know how much power you have so as not to go too far. I mean, I'm not a real feminine person like Dolly, but I'm not a bitch either. I don't make unreasonable demands because I've been raised to be considerate."

Tanya doesn't relate power to money as much as she does to talent. She's vague about money and surprisingly casual, especially since she went from so little to so much in such a short period of time. "Oh, sure, I like to spend money," she says in an offhand manner. "The band kids me when we pull into a new town. They start saying, 'Where's the mall? Where's the mall? Let Tanya out by the mall so she can spend some money!' They know how I love to shop around. But I buy something and wear it two or three times and then wonder why I ever bought it. What I do get a kick out of is buying things for other people. I bought my aunt a new Firebird the other day. It was the first new car she'd ever owned in her whole life, and it was great to see her face.

"My attorney sends me a weekly check—about two hundred dollars—for personal things, and the rest goes into a trust fund. I don't even know how much the check was for that I got from MCA. That's how much I know. If I want something big, like a new car or this farm, I just tell Dad and he gets the money for us. But the first time I read in a magazine that I was a millionaire—I was sixteen then—I didn't know who they were talking about for a minute. I had to stop and say, 'Hey, I guess I am.' But it didn't make me *feel* any different inside.

"The only time I really think about money," she says slowly, "is when I wonder what kind of man I'll fall in love with. My friends say, 'Lord, Tanya, you'll have to marry a millionaire,' or 'How will he feel about you having all that money?' And they may be right. It's degrading to a man for the wife to have all the money. My Dad says, 'When you get ready to marry, just tell him you've given all your money to me and you'll have to live off *his* income.'" She laughs. "But who wants to live off a normal income when you've got enough in the bank for a lifetime? That's why by the time I get married I want to have enough money put away to take care of my parents for the rest of their lives so I can ease back and just work when I want to."

This suggests that Tanya feels responsible for her parent's security, but she denies it defensively. "No, they've never made me feel responsible for them. They've worked as hard or harder for my career than I have, so whatever they get from it is money they've *earned*."

Tanya's personality is a lot like her singing— soft one minute, rough the next. As Beau says, "She lets a person know where they stand in a second."

"But it's gonna be hard for me to find a husband even without the money problem," Tanya says, slipping off the uncomfortable topic by changing the subject. "I mean, do you marry somebody in the business because they can understand your life better? That didn't work for Tammy and George. Or do you marry someone out of the business like Dolly did? That usually doesn't work either because there are so many demands made on your life, most husbands couldn't take it. Dolly's lucky. I think her husband is unique. He's not a bit interested in her career and never gets uptight about it.

"The problem is, of all the millions of men in the world, there are such a few *good* ones. And the kind of guys I like are the kind who are not the least impressed by me or my career. That type usually takes two or three weeks to get around to asking for a date and by that time I'm long gone. When you've only got a night or two in town you need a fast worker, and I hate fast workers. I like older men best, men in their late twenties or early thirties.

"My first boyfriend—he'll always be my first love—was a horse-trainer, and it was serious at the time but I don't know if you can really be in love that young. I still think about him, though. I was fourteen when I met him and I didn't even start dating till I was sixteen.

"Some kids would call me old-fashioned but I demand respect from a guy. That's why I wouldn't have sex with a man before I married him. I guess that's not my image because of my songs, but that's the way I feel. When I sing 'Will You Lay With Me' there are always a bunch of guys in the audience who yell out, 'Yeah, *yeah!*' " She laughs, blushing. "Once I even heard a *girl* saying 'Sure, baby' and I thought 'Hey wait a minute, what is *this?*' But it's just like I heard Dolly say once on a talk show. The host asked if her husband didn't mind her traveling all around the country alone with so many men out there and Dolly said, 'My husband knows I'm a lady.' From her looks a man might think she's fast, but if he talked to her five minutes he'd know different. From my songs

they might think I'm fast, but they find out different if they step out of line.

"If I went to bed with a guy I wasn't married to," she adds, "I wouldn't think he respected me and I know I wouldn't respect myself. I can't see it any other way." At times Tanya gives the impression that she says things she wants her father to see in print.

"One of the reasons teen-agers fool around so much sexually is because they're looking for the security they never got at home," she says. "I don't have to look for that. I'm not saying sex before marriage isn't okay for other people; I'm just saying it wouldn't work for me. Not just because I'm a celebrity, but because of my personality. It would be wrong for me to experiment with one-night stands because I think for a relationship to last it should take a little longer to get going.

"Fans might get the idea that I have a really exciting social life because of the places I go and the people I get to meet. But I have less dates, less *friends*, than they do because my work keeps me going all the time. That makes me appreciate real

Two very distinct sides of Tanya Tucker: Above, a 1977 Country Music Magazine shot complete with red satin sheets. "Official" Tanya photographs were very sophisticated during this period. Left, at sixteen, she enjoys a show with some friends.

friends all the more. Seals and Croft were in town recently and we had so much fun together, I thought, 'Other people take it for granted to go out to dinner and a movie with good friends, but it's so unusual for me, it's a real *thrill*.' Just sitting around talking about things like religion—they're into Baha'i and I'm mixed up about religion right now so it was interesting to listen to people with firm opinions—or talking about movies or music was really exciting. I'm used to getting my thrills from the stage, not from my personal life."

Tanya admits readily, agreeing with Loretta, that what happens to a performer on stage is the bottom line to the whole business. "Performing is my reward for all the hard work that goes on before and after," she says. "Oh, there are other thrills—like meeting idols—but once you've met that person, the thrill is gone forever. Like when I met Elvis it was terrific. I was sitting in the audience in Las Vegas with Costa and he said from the stage, 'There's a lady out there who's one of the prettiest in country music.' " Tanya imitates Elvis' voice as she relates the story. "And

Various stages of Tanya: Below, the Amazing Voice at fourteen; far right, the Female Elvis; near right, the young sophisticate (1977).

I'm punching Costa and going 'Oh, God,' and she's going 'Oh, God' and we're having a fit. He introduced me and my knees were shaking so hard I could barely stand up. Then we got to go backstage and it was like a dream come true. He was as nice as I'd hoped he would be.

"Then Steve McQueen and Ali MacGraw came to see me at the Palomino in North Hollywood and that was a thrill. We didn't get to talk much because the photographers and reporters wouldn't leave them alone, but just finding out they were fans of *mine* was a thrill.

"Everytime I break a house record it's a thrill. Like I broke the one at the Pal [the Palomino Club in Los Angeles], and we broke the record in Salt Lake City recently. Lynn Anderson had performed there the day before and we blew her away. In Pueblo we beat Helen Reddy, Mac Davis and Johnny Cash's records and we almost beat the Osmonds.

"But once you've met the idol or broken the record, you can't do that again, so the thrill is gone forever. On stage it's different. The thrill is just as good anytime it's right. Sometimes you feel it before you even get to the stage. You pull into the auditorium parking lot and you see thousands of cars and you say, 'Wow, they all came here to see *me*. Man, what a thing!' And you can hear them from backstage and when you walk out there and the applause hits you . . . I can't really describe it. But it's probably the best feeling in the world. Then when you finish and you start to come off the stage and the kids are screaming and hands are reaching up, wanting to touch you, and you feel . . . *powerful*. Yes, powerful. But at the same time you want to give *them* something. You know you've gotten it all back in that one night—not counting the twenty or thirty thousand you just made—and you say to yourself, 'Man, I just got paid.' That's what keeps an artist going,

keeps them on the road in front of the people. You get addicted to the thrill, because it's the only one you can keep having over and over."

Tanya's drive and ambition have never faltered nor diminished during her rise to stardom. If anything she is more determined than ever to "go all the way . . . as far as my talent will take me." But one thing has changed. For the first time in her life, Tanya is afraid.

"I understand why I'm afraid of getting older," she says softly, measuring her words carefully. "I had such a good childhood I'm in no hurry to leave it. But I'm also beginning to have fears about my career that I never used to feel. I'm just beginning to realize how many responsibilities I have . . . how many people depend on me to earn a living. I used to think of singing just in terms of pleasing myself, because I'm such a perfectionist. But as I get older I realize more and more that this thing I call a career is more than just singing, putting on a good show, making good records. It's a way of *life* for a lot of people, and the weight of that responsibility scares me sometimes. I can handle it, but I don't know why it's just now hitting me that it's something to think about, not something you can take for granted."

Tanya pauses for a moment, then sighs, half to herself. "I guess this is what they call growing up, and I'm not at all sure I'm gonna like it!" she says.

Then she brightens as suddenly as a child who's just heard the recess bell. "But one thing's for sure. It'll be fun to see how I turn out. Right now I'm about nine different people. As soon as you think you know one, another pops out. I haven't found my own style yet in my music, or in myself either. But when I do, I'll know it, 'cause it'll *feel* right, and I'll probably look back and say, 'Who was that kid who didn't want to grow up? Boy, am I glad *she's* not around anymore!'" ♥

PHOTO CREDITS

p. 9: Raeanne Rubenstein
p. 10: Alan Whitman, Yvonne Hanneman (r)
p. 11: Raeanne Rubenstein
p. 13: Raeanne Rubenstein
p. 15: Raeanne Rubenstein
p. 16: Raeanne Rubenstein
p. 17: Alan Whitman
p. 18: Courtesy Loretta Lynn,
    Courtesy of the CMF (top r)
p. 19: Courtesy of Loretta Lynn
p. 22: John Lee
p. 23: John Lee, Raeanne Rubenstein
p. 24: Raeanne Rubenstein
p. 25: Courtesy Loretta Lynn
p. 26: Raeanne Rubenstein
p. 29: Courtesy Loretta Lynn
p. 31: Raeanne Rubenstein (bottom l.)
    Courtesy Loretta Lynn
p. 33: Raeanne Rubenstein
p. 35: Marshall Fallwell, Jr.
p. 36: John Lee (r), courtesy CBS Records
p. 37: Courtesy CBS Records
p. 39: Courtesy Tammy Wynette
p. 40: Alan Whitman
p. 41: Courtesy CBS Records
p. 42: Courtesy CBS Records
p. 44: Courtesy CBS Records
p. 45: Raeanne Rubenstein
p. 47: Raeanne Rubenstein
p. 48: Courtesy Tammy Wynette
p. 50: Courtesy CBS Records
p. 51: Leonard Kamsler
p. 53: Marshall Fallwell, Jr.
p. 54: Raeanne Rubenstein
p. 57: Raeanne Rubenstein (bottom l.),
    courtesy CBS Records
p. 59: Raeanne Rubenstein
p. 61: Courtesy CBS Records
p. 63: Michael G. Borum
p. 64: Alan Whitman (r), courtesy CMF
p. 65: Courtesy the CMF
p. 67: Marshall Fallwell, Jr.
p. 68: Alan Whitman
p. 69: Alan Whitman
p. 70: Courtesy the CMF
p. 71: Courtesy the CMF
p. 72: Alan Whitman
p. 73: Alan Whitman

p. 75: Courtesy the House of Cash
p. 76: Courtesy the House of Cash
p. 79: Michael G. Borum
p. 81: Michael G. Borum
p. 82: Michael G. Borum
p. 83: Michael G. Borum
p. 85: Raeanne Rubenstein
p. 86: Michael G. Borum
p. 87: Alan Whitman
p. 89: Raeanne Rubenstein
p. 91: Alan Whitman
p. 93: Michael G. Borum
p. 94: Raeanne Rubenstein (r), courtesy Dolly Parton
p. 96: Michael G. Borum
p. 98: Hope Powell (inset), courtesy Dolly Parton
p. 100: Courtesy Dolly Parton
p. 101: Courtesy Dolly Parton
p. 102: Raeanne Rubenstein
p. 103: John Lee
p. 105: Leonard Kamsler
p. 108: Raeanne Rubenstein
p. 109: Raeanne Rubenstein
p. 111: Raeanne Rubenstein, Michael G. Borum, John Lee
p. 112: Courtesy RCA Records
p. 115: Hope Powell, Raeanne Rubenstein
p. 116: John Lee
P. 117: John Lee, Marshall Fallwell, Jr. (bottom)
p. 118: Raeanne Rubenstein
p. 119: Michael G. Borum
p. 121: Raeanne Rubenstein
p. 123: Leonard Kamsler
p. 124: Raeanne Rubenstein
p. 125: Raeanne Rubenstein
p. 126: Courtesy Tanya Tucker
p. 129: John Lee
p. 131: Raeanne Rubenstein
p. 132: Courtesy Tanya Tucker
p. 133: Leonard Kamsler,
    Courtesy CBS Records, Raeanne Rubenstein
p. 137: Emerson-Loew
p. 138: Courtesy Tanya Tucker
p. 140: Emerson-Loew
p. 142: Raeanne Rubenstein
p. 144: Raeanne Rubenstein
p. 145: Leonard Kamsler
p. 146: Courtesy Tanya Tucker, Leonard Kamsler
p. 147: John Lee
p. 149: Leonard Kamsler

Note: 'CMF' is an abbreviation of The Country Music Foundation Library and Media Center